HELPING PARENTS COPE WITH CHILDREN'S ADJUSTMENT PROBLEMS

ABOUT THE AUTHORS

Gary A. Crow is Executive Director of Lorain County Children Services in Elyria, Ohio. Letha I. Crow is an independent consultant and trainer. Dr. and Mrs. Crow have consulted and trained extensively for schools, mental health, and social services agencies, police departments, Head Start programs, churches, YMCA and other youth programs, and for a variety of professional and civic groups. Mrs. Crow has served on the faculty of Urbana University; and Dr. Crow has been on the faculties of several universities including The Ohio State University and The Methodist Theological School In Ohio. Other publications by the Crows include *Crisis Intervention And Suicide Prevention,* and *The Functioning Of The Family System* published by Charles C Thomas Publishers, and *Our Home—Your Home* and *A Common Sense Guide To Culture And Foster Care* published by American Foster Care Resources. The Crows live in Elyria, Ohio.

HELPING PARENTS COPE WITH CHILDREN'S ADJUSTMENT PROBLEMS

An Advice-Giving Guide For Professionals

By

GARY A. CROW, PH.D.
LETHA I. CROW, M.S.W.

CHARLES C THOMAS • PUBLISHER, LTD.
Springfield • Illinois • U.S.A.

Published and Distributed Throughout the World by

CHARLES C THOMAS • PUBLISHER, LTD.
2600 South First Street
Springfield, Illinois 62794-9265

ISBN 0-398-06725-2 (cloth)
ISBN 0-398-06726-0 (paper)

Library of Congress Catalog Card Number: 96-32540

With THOMAS BOOKS *careful attention is given to all details of manufacturing and design. It is the Publisher's desire to present books that are satisfactory as to their physical qualities and artistic possibilities and appropriate for their particular use.* THOMAS BOOKS *will be true to those laws of quality that assure a good name and good will.*

Printed in the United States of America
SC-R-3

Library of Congress Cataloging-in-Publication Data

Crow, Gary A., 1942–
Helping parents cope with children's adjustment problems : an advice giving guide for professionals / by Gary A. Crow, Letha I. Crow.
p. cm.
Includes bibliographical references.
ISBN 0-398-06725-2 (cloth)
1. Mental health consultation. 2. Adjustment disorders in children. 3. Parents—Counseling of. I. Crow, Letha I. II. Title.
RJ503.45.C76 1996
618.92'89—dc20 96-32540
CIP

PREFACE

Parents ask professionals from many disciplines for advice about how to cope with their children's adjustment problems. They frequently turn to teachers and other school personnel, ministers, police and juvenile officers, recreation and youth leaders, nurses, social workers in non-mental health practices, physicians not specializing in childhood difficulties, and a wide variety of other helping professionals whose expertise is not specifically in childhood maladjustment. This advice giving guide will enable these professionals to:

- Better understand childhood maladjustment;
- Appropriately and effectively advise parents whose children are having adjustment problems related to:
  - Stress;
  - Depression, including signs related to suicide;
  - Learning difficulties, especially those that result in children's having adjustment problems at school;
  - Serious behavior problems, considering both the variety of behavior problems and the progressive development of behavior disorders;
  - Interpersonal maladjustment, including identifying and understanding the signs commonly associated with social adjustment problems;
  - Mental illness, including the signs most typically exhibited by seriously emotionally disturbed young people;
  - Medically related symptoms, including some tips and suggestions about their urgency and when they require the attention of a physician.

Children are complex, multi-dimensional people whose potentials and problems can only be fully understood within the context of their interdependent physical, emotional, moral, social, sexual, and intellectual dimensions. The development and adjustment of young people are similarly complex processes that require sensitivity, understanding, and much patience. Their parents need to be proactive, involved people who envision a fulfilling future for their kids and understand that today's behavior and adjustment are shaping that future. Your challenge is to help them understand their roles and associated responsibilities and to knowledgeably and appropriately support their efforts. We have made our best effort to provide you with the most essential information we think you will need to successfully fill this important role. Our hope is that you accept the challenge and that the sensitive and thoughtful advice you provide to parents enriches their lives and the lives of their children.

G.A.C., L.I.C.

ACKNOWLEDGMENTS

Completion of *Helping Parents Cope With Children's Adjustment Problems* is not an event but is rather the most recent iteration of an ongoing process. For over thirty years, the authors have focused most of their professional interest and energy on achieving excellence for children and their families and on consulting with and learning from others whose dedication is to the same outcome. One benefit of this pursuit has been the opportunity to know and work with professionals from many disciplines who have diverse perspectives, varying theoretical orientations, individual expertise, and distinct styles and approaches. The common thread within this eclecticism is a passion for success for young people and their families. To whatever extent this book contributes to that success, those with whom we have worked and from whom we have learned certainly must share the credit.

In addition to extending our appreciation to those who have knowingly and unknowingly contributed to our knowledge and understanding through the years, we are especially pleased to acknowledge the contributions of six people to this project.

Jacob R. Sprouse, Jr. with American Foster Care Resources; King George, Virginia was the editor and publisher of *Our Home – Your Home,* a foster parent training curriculum that incorporates many of the concepts in this book specifically as they relate to foster parenting with abused and neglected children. Mr. Sprouse also supported a survey-based research project that confirms that the "signs" of maladjustment in children included here are not culturally linked, i.e., the signs are indicators of maladjustment when seen in any child, regardless of the cultural background of the child. A training curriculum for foster parents, using the findings of that research was published by AFCR and is titled *A Common Sense Guide To Culture And Foster Care.*

Jeannie Weisbrod, M.S.W., has worked with us on the conceptualization and development of the book and has made many suggestions that have significantly increased its accuracy, completeness, and readability.

Barbara Hill-Newby, Ph.D., reviewed the manuscript with attention to conceptual clarity and to the completeness of the advice that is offered for the book's readers and for the parents with whom they will be talking.

Delbert Mason, M.D., provided significant insight and expertise with the medical aspects of the book, especially with the "Common Medical Concerns" in Chapter 8.

Jane Robertson, M.S.S.A., reviewed the manuscript and made several suggestions that have improved its usefulness for "other experts."

Joan Allsop provided invaluable assistance with assuring that the manuscript was correctly formatted and free from typing errors. She also tested the book against a "Does it make sense?" standard from the perspective of the general reader.

Of course, the authors are responsible for the book and its content and those who have generously added their expertise to it are not responsible for any shortcomings or inadequacies in the final product. This not withstanding, their contributions are sincerely appreciated.

CONTENTS

HELPING PARENTS COPE WITH CHILDREN'S ADJUSTMENT PROBLEMS

CHAPTER 1

INTRODUCTION

Overview

Do parents[1] request your advice about difficulties their children are having? Do you observe young people and notice signs of maladjustment? Do you occasionally take the initiative to discuss your concerns with the parents of the youngsters with whom you work? Do parents *think of you as an expert in the area of child maladjustment,* though your expertise is not specifically in that area? If so, *"Helping Parents Cope With Children's Adjustment Problems"* is a guide for you.

Specialists from many disciplines are asked for advice by parents who are concerned about their children. Because of their positions, these professionals may notice that youngsters are having difficulties before parents request their advice. Child psychologists, child psychiatrists, pediatricians, social workers in child guidance centers, and similar experts are normally the best resources for maladjusted children and their families. Nonetheless, they are not the people with whom parents first talk; and they are usually not in positions to initially notice signs of maladjustment. Rather, they see the children only after other experts have identified the potential difficulty, have discussed it with the youngster's parents, and have made a referral to a specialist.

Who are these other experts? They represent many professions and include teachers and other school personnel, ministers, police and juvenile officers, recreation and youth leaders, nurses, social workers in non-mental health practices, physicians not specializing in childhood difficulties, and a wide variety of other helping professionals. Many of these other experts specialize in areas including some aspects of children's adjustment and development but are not experts in the broader area of childhood maladjustment.

---

[1]The term "parents" is intended to include the child's biological parents, single parents, stepparents, or any other adults who have primary responsibility for the development, adjustment, and well-being of the child.

For example, teachers are experts in the areas of learning and education but may not be as comfortable with emotional and behavior problems. Youth ministers are experts in the area of spiritual development and adjustment but typically are not as well trained in the areas of childhood stress, depression, or learning disorders.

This book is a guide for those other experts so that the quality and appropriateness of the advice they give will have a comprehensive perspective and maximum effectiveness. It is not a substitute for timely referrals to qualified specialists but is instead a guide for other experts whose advice is now and then requested. The book will enable you to better advise the parents who turn to you for support and guidance and expand your understanding of maladjustment in the children with whom you work.

Parents' Active Role

Parents want their children to become healthy, effective, successful adults. This assumption is so seldom invalid that you may simply take it for granted. As you focus parents' attention on this outcome for their children, your first task is to help them clarify their ideas about what qualities make an effective and successful adult. This vision for their children's future is the foundation on which their active involvement rests.

Effective parents are not passive individuals who from time to time intervene into the lives of their children. Rather, they are proactive, involved people who envision a fulfilling future for their kids and understand that today's behavior and adjustment are shaping that future. Their challenge is to energetically encourage and support those qualities in their children that characterize success in adults. Conversely, those qualities and characteristics they believe are not desirable and that are not found in effective and successful adults need to be thoughtfully discouraged as their children grow.

Most adult characteristics, good or bad, are seen in children at some stage in their development. Small children, for example, take things that do not belong to them. In adults, the same behavior is called stealing. Young children misrepresent what has happened and do not always tell their parents how things really are. In adults, this behavior is called lying. Children are naturally loving and affectionate; and through their parents' nurturing, they likely will still be that way when they are grown.

Kids also are spontaneous and enthusiastic, qualities similarly desirable in adults. Behavior and characteristics that are desirable or undesirable in adults need to be encouraged or discouraged as children grow and mature.[2] You can assist parents who request your advice by facilitating their thinking carefully through these important issues. As their confidant, you are in a good position to help them focus on the importance of their playing an active role in the lives of their kids.

Development

Children have a physical, doing dimension. It incorporates their physical bodies, their potentials and capacities to do and behave, and most of what is visible in terms of their actions and activities. Part of each parent's role is to help his or her children grow to respect and appreciate their physical abilities and skills, to know how to behave in a variety of situations, and to recognize and utilize their physical capacities and potentials. This physical, doing dimension starts at infancy and is central to kids' adjustment throughout their ongoing, on-growing journey to adulthood.

The same level of importance holds for the emotional dimension of children. Here are found feelings, fears and frustrations, sadness and joy, disappointment and excitement, love and hate, fun and futility. Growing children experience all of these emotions and need to learn how to interpret them, how to express them, and how to manage them. For example, kids must learn to express anger without having tantrums, to deal with despair and disappointment without becoming destructively depressed, to express love and joy without getting into harmful or inappropriate relationships. Within this dimension, children must learn to deal with the internal experience of emotions as well as how to express their feelings effectively and appropriately.

Around the age of four or five the moral, spiritual dimension begins to emerge. Effectively helping children develop a solid sense of right and wrong, good and bad, requires that their parents are clear about their own values and beliefs in these areas. Success in this dimension is critical to success in the social dimension that emerges about the same

[2]At times, a child's behavior may only be inappropriate or undesirable by degree. For example, aggression is often a problem because of its intensity or how it is expressed. For some behavior, the need is to channel or shape the behavior and not to eliminate it. It is important to help parents make this distinction.

time. When kids are about five or six, the social dimension becomes dominate and begins to interact with the other developing dimensions. The social dimension embraces the child's potential to interact with other children and adults and to become socially effective and self-determined.

By about eleven or twelve, the young person's emerging sexual dimension begins dynamically interacting with the other developing dimensions. Sexual behavior and attitudes that are appropriate and inappropriate, healthy and unhealthy, effective and ineffective are best conveyed to maturing adolescents by parents who have thought through the issues.[3]

This central parental responsibility similarly applies to the thinking, learning dimension that starts at birth and gains focus at seventeen or eighteen. By then, young people need to be self-directed, skilled learners who are formulating independent ideas and perceptions and who can think critically, clearly, and thoroughly. Older adolescents should be receptive to the ideas of others and at the same time be able to combine those ideas with their own, i.e., they should be thinking for themselves.

Clearly, an important aspect of your advice for parents is for them to conscientiously think through their expectations for their children physically, emotionally, morally and spiritually, socially, sexually, and intellectually. The multidimensionality of their kids requires and deserves nothing less.

The Learning Process

Children first discover and then experiment with what they have discovered. They then repeat the activity, action, behavior, or experience until they have either mastered it or determined that it has no value for them. When children achieve mastery, their knowledge and skills become conscious: they use the knowledge or skill when it is needed for the sake of something else.

Language development illustrates this progression both in terms of the process and the ongoing nature of learning. A child discovers the

[3]For younger children, "sexual" behavior normally is not related to interests and interactions associated with "adult" sexuality. Rather, it is related to physical and gender interest and curiosity. If "adult" interests or specifically "sexual" content is present, a specialized consultation is indicated to assess possible sexual abuse or inappropriate sexual experience.

possibility of making noises and gestures. As he[4] experiments with making sounds, he soon learns that people respond in different ways to different noises. Once his skill has developed to the point where people usually respond in the expected way, a specific verbalization or gesture can be consciously used.

Throughout childhood and adult life, though, people continually discover new verbalizations and gestures. With each discovery, the process of experimentation leading to mastery comes into play. With adolescents and adults, the experimentation/mastery phase with new words and gestures is very brief and requires little attention; but from young children, parents receive endless questions and requests mixed with a very frustrating flow of verbalizations and gestures. Most parents notice that, despite consistent responses, their child may continue asking the same question, making the same gesture, or verbalizing in the same way. The child is experimenting: Is the parental response predictable or will the answer change?

This pattern of discovery, experimentation, and mastery leading to conscious use can be seen in most learning.

Parents tell their three-year-old that he has made a pretty picture. They are then inundated with pretty pictures. They tell their nine-year-old that his way of doing something won't work. He persists, nonetheless, until his experiments convince him it will not work. Once in a while, his way does work and he learns that usually his parents are right but occasionally they are wrong.

A child's learning is continuous and follows a fairly predictable course. It starts with discoveries that lead to experimentation, which in turn lead to further discoveries and more experimentation. Through this repeating and expanding process, growing children gradually come to master a wide range of knowledge and many skills. As their physical, emotional, and social abilities expand, they discover new possibilities within things they had relegated to conscious use.

Learning is ever dynamic, ongoing, expanding, and exciting. Effective parents encourage such learning while ineffective parents tend to discourage it.

The process of discovery leading to experimentation also suggests that

---

[4]Unless inappropriate in an example-specific context, male pronouns are primarily used. This avoids the repetitious use of he/she, his/her, etc. Nonetheless, all materials apply to boys and girls, unless specifically noted.

children seldom learn the first time they have an experience, the first time they are told about something, the first time they discover that things sometimes do not work or sometimes turn out badly. Likewise, their parents' initial efforts to teach them about most anything may not be effective. Children often need to experiment with parental ideas and pronouncements before they decide to integrate them into their view of things.

Parents sometimes overlook the reality that they are learning along with their kids. You can help them see that, before their responses become internalized by their children, they will have ample opportunities to try again, when necessary. They can say to their child:

- "Let me tell you this again."
- "I was wrong."
- "I made a mistake."
- "I overreacted."
- "I didn't do that right."
- "What I told you was incorrect."

They and their children are learning together. Along with this shared learning, the parents are modeling for their kids appropriate mistake-making behavior. Neither they nor their children have to always be right, have to be perfect. It is enough to try their best, sometimes fail, learn through experience, and try again. Learning is a three steps forward and two steps back kind of thing sometimes. Both parents and their children need to understand, accept, and value the process itself and not give too much importance to where they are in the learning process at any specific time.

Reader's Guide

The foregoing introduction sets the stage for the following eight chapters. As a specialist whose expertise is not specifically with maladjusted children, you have seen that it is important to clarify with parents their expectations for their children and to help them understand and accept the active and involved role they must play if their kids are to succeed. Too often, parents take a passive position, deferring to experts and behaving as if they expect those experts to "fix" their children. Of course, this cannot happen. Helping youngsters through periods of maladjustment is a collaborative, shared process in which parents must actively participate, if it is to be effective. Central to the outcome are the parents' expectations and goals for their children and their commitment to actively work on that outcome. Your challenge is to help them understand their roles and associated responsibilities and to support their efforts.

An important part of your task is to teach parents to appropriately and sensitively interact with their kids as they work through the issues and concerns for which they are seeking your advice. The examples and illustrations you will be considering incorporate an approach that emphasizes the following essential, child-friendly behaviors:

- Parents honestly sharing their feelings and perceptions with their children,
- Parents modeling appropriate communication, problem solving, and interpersonal management skills,
- Parents openly and candidly letting their children know how the kids' behavior and patterns of adjustment are effecting the parents and others in the family,
- Parents clearly communicating to their children that they sincerely care about them and about what they think and feel,
- Parents consistently providing emotional and interpersonal support and security for their children,
- Parents helping their children fully understand the short and long-term implications of not acknowledging and dealing with their problems,[5]
- Parents assuring their children that there is help for the kids' problems and that they can and will help them get the help they need,
- Parents empowering their children to make choices about the help they will receive and to play an active role in identifying, understanding, and working on what may be the most important issues and opportunities in their lives.

In the preceding sections, you also have seen that children are complex, multidimensional people whose potentials and problems can only be fully understood within the context of their interdependent physical, emotional, moral, social, sexual, and intellectual dimensions. Your success with facilitating parents' understanding this multi-dimensional per-

[5]It is important for you to help parents be sure that they understand the short and long-term implications of not dealing with their child's problems as a prerequisite to their helping him understand.

spective is key to their seeking and accepting the advice you will offer and following through with the referrals you may make to specialists. The same idea applies to their understanding of how their kids learn. You can help them see that learning is a process that takes time and much patience. It is additionally taking place within each developing dimension. This means, for example, that what kids do, what they say, and how they feel about it do not match up very well at times.

Parents say, "It makes no sense to me at all."

Your developing understanding helps you say, "It's confusing. It looks like it may be as confusing to your child as it is to you. Maybe a place to begin understanding is to talk with your child to see where she is with what happened and with what she thinks and what she feels about it.[6] The most important part of it is to let her know that you want to think and feel with her about things. Let her know you're confused and are ready to listen and to help her get on with getting on. She needs to know that you are in her corner and will still be there, no matter what."

The next seven chapters help you recognize, understand, and assist parents with many of the most common signs of maladjustment in children. Chapter 2 focuses on signs of stress; and Chapter 3 draws your attention to signs of depression, including signs related to suicide. Chapter 4 is devoted to signs of learning problems, especially those that cause youngsters difficulty in school.

Chapter 5 covers the most common signs of serious behavior maladjustment and helps you consider both the variety of behavior problems and the progressive development of behavior disorders. In Chapter 6 you will read about socially maladjusted kids and learn to identify and understand the signs commonly associated with social adjustment problems. Mental illness in children and the signs most typically exhibited by seriously emotionally disturbed young people are presented in Chapter 7.

Common medical concerns are listed in Chapter 8, including some tips and suggestions about their urgency and when they require the attention of a physician. Chapter 9 closes the book with some final thoughts about parental maladjustment and how to facilitate parents' receiving the expert help they may themselves need.

---

[6]The parents need to see the world in general and their child's problems specifically from her point of view. It is axiomatic that helping children must start from their perspective. Always start where the child is.

Let us leave you to your journey through the book with two cautions and a recommendation. First, this book is a guide and is not a substitute for in-depth training and expertise. You will be able to better assist parents in identifying, understanding, and handling their children's problems but will not, by reading this book, become the "best choice" for ongoing, in-depth help if those problems persist or are serious. Second, you should never share your conclusions with parents based on only considering a single sign or unique situation. The following chapters will help you first put the sign or situation into a more general context while identifying possibly related signs and problems. This will enable you to discuss parents' concerns in terms of broader categories such as stress, learning difficulty, or serious social maladjustment. This perspective helps parents think in terms of problem areas and underlying issues instead of focusing on a specific behavior or circumstance. If you only accomplish this much with them, you have provided an invaluable service that will directly benefit their child.

Our recommendation is this. Although you will get the most this book has to offer by carefully reading it all the way through, you will be well-served if you at least skim through all the chapters before skipping to specific chapters or sections. A central strength of the book is its comprehensive and systematic approach to maladjustment in kids. Without familiarizing yourself with the book's scope, you will miss a good learning opportunity. Also, you run the risk of overlooking important signs of maladjustment that you may not have thought to consider. This is especially true since many of the signs throughout the book are interrelated, requiring your having a broad perspective from which to help parents avoid over or underinterpreting specific signs.

We have made our best effort to provide you with the most important information we think you will need to function in your role as an "other expert." If you need more information, we encourage you to consider the book's bibliography and to access your local library for additional reading on a specific topic. Additionally, school psychologists, pediatricians, professionals at local mental health or child guidance clinics, staff members of family service agencies, and individuals in private practice are usually willing to provide a telephone consultation about a child free of charge. If you are not sure who to call, try the nursing or social services departments at the nearest hospital. Police officers, teachers, ministers, and professionals in other "helping" professions also are usually able to assist you with identifying area experts in childhood maladjustment. The key is to identify a specialist whose expertise is in the specific area in which you and the child's parents have identified potential problems.

CHAPTER 2

STRESS

Overview

Stress is normally not a significant problem for children. Kids can normally think things through and figure them out for themselves, despite some stress. They can usually handle their feelings whether they are feeling good or not and can do what they need to do. They have some stress but handle it fine. Nonetheless, children may experience more stress than they can comfortably handle. When they do, there are normally observable signs that their stress is getting to them. Listen to Cathy's internal struggle as she tries to mentally manage her building stress and then visualize her behavior as she abruptly leaves the room.

> Cathy is feeling very restless and cannot get herself to calm down. She cannot concentrate on anything and is feeling the start of a headache. The past few nights, she tossed and turned for what seemed like hours before falling asleep. Last night, she woke up several times and it took forever to go back to sleep. Waking up was not that bad; but the bad dreams upset her and kept her from going back to sleep. She could not get them off her mind.
>
> "Calm down," Cathy tells herself. "I think I'm going to be sick." She thinks her upset stomach is because of something she ate but the more upset she gets, the worse it gets. "Don't start crying again. I've got to get out of here," she screams to herself. Between her upset stomach and a growing headache, there is no way she can pay attention to what her mother is saying. Without a word, Cathy turns and bolts out of the room.

Signs of Stress

The following questions highlight common signs of stress parents may mention to you and about which they may want your advice. Even if they are not of specific concern to the parents, you should still ask if their child is having any of these problems. This will facilitate your developing a broad perspective for the advice you will offer. You are initiating the process of exploring multiple areas within which signs of maladjustment and potential causes of those difficulties may be identified.

Explore with the parents whether their youngster has had the problem within the past week or so. If not, go to the next question. If he has experienced the problem, put a check mark beside the question and then go to the next question. Repeat the process until they have considered each question.

Does Their Child:

- Become restless and unable to calm down?
- Have unusual trouble concentrating and paying attention?
- Take more than an hour to go to sleep or awakened during the night, taking more than a half hour to go back to sleep?
- Have bad dreams or nightmares?
- Have headaches?
- Have trouble with an upset stomach?
- Cry for no apparent reason or had crying spells?
- Lose his temper with little or no provocation?

If none of the questions were checked, the likelihood is that stress is not a significant problem for the child at this time. If one or more questions has been checked, there may be stress-related difficulties. The following sections will help you determine whether problematic stress is present, facilitate your helping the child's parents pinpoint the issues, and enable you to appropriately advise them.

Restlessness and Trouble Calming Down

Children can be restless and unable to calm down when they are just full of energy. They are only being very active. It is really hard to sit still, stand still, or be still. Their problem is not stress, it is having to be calm and quiet.

School and the dinner table are good examples. The only stress is adults who expect them to quit fooling around. The children are just being children. The adults are the ones with the stress.

When restlessness and trouble calming down are because of stress, it does not feel good. The young person is having thoughts and feelings that are keeping him upset. He is confused and feels afraid, angry, and frustrated at the same time. He cannot manage these thoughts and feelings very well and is uptight and uneasy.

If this sign is present for the child, encourage his parents to think about whether their child has a problem or if perhaps they are simply having difficulty coping with his energy and normal behavior. If the issue actually reflects parental stress, encourage them to share *their problem* with him. They might say, "I want to talk with you about slowing down and settling down a little, especially at dinner and when we're having quiet time in the evening. You're too noisy; and I find it hard to handle."

If you think the child may be restless and having trouble calming down because of stress, encourage his parents to offer to talk with him about whatever is bothering him, to assure him that they want to try to help him if he wants, and then to give him a little more space. They often may simply need to be more patient and tolerant. It also helps for parents to understand that children usually handle the big stresses in their lives fairly well; and parents normally know what those are. It is the little stresses that build and accumulate for children, as they do for adults. Understanding this facilitates parents' being more patient, not expecting their child to specifically know what is bothering him, and giving him more personal and emotional freedom to work through his unique stresses.

They might say, "I can tell you have a lot on your mind. I'll give you as much time and space as you need to work it out. If you want to talk, I'm here for you."

If he is not noticeably more relaxed in a day or so, they should become somewhat more insistent. They might say, "Whatever you are struggling with seems like a big problem for you. I can't tell whether you are winning or if whatever is bothering you is winning. It's time to talk. Let me help. I know the two of us can handle any problem better than either of us by ourselves. Can we talk?"

If he refuses to talk, they need to keep trying, not right then but from time to time and at least once a day. Support them in not becoming frustrated and uptight just because he will not talk to them. Helping a youngster with stress can be stressful. Nonetheless, it is important for his parents to model good stress management behavior.

Trouble Concentrating and Paying Attention

This sign of stress is a lot like restlessness and trouble calming down; but it is more of a problem for the youngster. Some children (about one in twenty) have a condition called Attention Deficit Hyperactivity Disorder or ADHD. These young people have abnormal problems concentrating and paying attention. Though this probably is not their child's problem, be sure his parents consider the possibility. If their child has ADHD, he can do nothing about it by himself and his parents will likely be ineffective as they try to deal with him. Only a pediatrician and child psychologist working in collaboration with the child's parents and teachers can diagnose ADHD with certainty. It then needs managed medically, behaviorally, and through special teaching and learning techniques. Importantly, simply prescribing medication without other types of behavior and learning interventions is an incomplete and inadequate response. There may be short-term benefits; but achieving long-term benefits requires a multi-disciplinary approach. The child and his parents cannot successfully cope with ADHD without this type of cooperative approach.

At home and school, problems concentrating and paying attention often are read wrong by adults. They read them as daydreaming and willfully not paying attention. A parent might tell you, "She spends all her time daydreaming, not paying attention, fooling around, and wasting time." When misread this way, a serious stress problem can be easily overlooked. If this happens, the child is more likely to be punished than helped.

Ask parents who are feeling frustrated by their child's behavior to think about this. Have they ever had to be somewhere that was uninteresting, boring, and no fun? What if it were even worse? They have trouble understanding anything being said and do not know what is happening. Be sure they get the picture.

Now, what if the parents are told that it is important and good for them? What if they are told that they will understand how important it really is in ten or twenty or thirty years? What if they are told that they will be in big trouble if they do not pay attention and make the most of the opportunity? What will it take to get the parents to concentrate and pay attention? Most children are in these kinds of situations often and do about as well or as badly as their parents. Before they take any action, parents should think about how reasonable they are being when they expect their child to concentrate and pay attention.

Most children who have trouble concentrating and paying attention because of stress are ignored. Even worse for them, they are treated as if they were misbehaving. What's more, parents often think they were misbehaving on purpose.

Help the youngster's parents to look for underlying causes and explanations. If their child often has trouble concentrating and paying attention, ADHD needs to be considered. If the problem mostly comes up at school or when their child needs to listen carefully or read, a learning disability may be part of his maladjustment problem. A school or child psychologist is the best resource for evaluating the possibility of learning problems. If, alternatively, the sign mostly occurs when the youngster has no choice about where to be or what to do, encourage his parents to think about how hard it is for him to pretend to be interested or to act like he cares when he does not.

If the problem suddenly comes up or especially if it had been there but is getting worse, stress is the most likely cause. The child's parents need to talk with him about their concerns. The conversation might, for example, start like this.

"I'm concerned about you. It seems like you're having trouble concentrating and paying attention. I noticed this when you were working on your homework, just as an example. It seems like you have a lot on your mind. It's hard to concentrate when we're thinking about important stuff. It's a problem for me sometimes, too. Can we talk about what's getting to you?"

If the youngster does not want to talk, this follow-up sometimes helps. "Let me try again. I respect the fact that you don't want to talk about whatever is bothering you. Here's my problem. I'm worried and am uncomfortable just letting go of it. If you really want me to back off, I will; but I'll feel better if you can share just a little with me about what's got you so upset."

If the child chooses to talk some, encourage his parents to listen, acknowledge his feelings, and resist any temptation to criticize, give uninvited advice, or tell him that he is getting upset over "nothing." He is the judge of what is stressful for him. If he feels stressed, it is stressful. It is as simple as that. If their child continues not to talk and especially if he becomes angry or withdraws, they need to keep some emotional and physical distance but check back with him every day or two to see how he is doing.

Trouble Going to Sleep or Awakening During the Night

This sign is usually not particularly important unless it goes on for a while. Children normally go to sleep in about fifteen minutes to an hour. The average is approximately twenty minutes or so. Some youngsters go to sleep quickly and others take longer to settle and fall asleep. It is only a problem if it takes a lot longer than is typical for the specific child. If this happens several nights in a row or if the youngster cannot fall asleep for three or four hours some night, there might be a problem. Excitement, not feeling tired, and thinking about day-to-day things can keep children awake as they can adults. Be sure parents are not making too much of it unless their child's sleeping problem is severe or persistent. Still, they need to be open to the possibility of too much stress.

Waking up during the night once in a while is not a problem either. Everyone does this sometimes. Usually, it is from dreaming or from needing to go to the bathroom. Not going back to sleep fairly quickly is more of a problem. When the youngster often wakes up but cannot go back to sleep easily, stress is the likely cause.

If their school-age child's sleeping does not improve in two weeks, suggest that the parents arrange for a medical evaluation. This may lead to the physician's recommending counseling. For younger children, a week is long enough to justify concern. When a child is taking his stress to bed with him, he needs some extra help.

Bad Dreams and Nightmares

Stress can be a problem for children all the time or just once in a while. It also can be mild or more serious. As it gets worse, the child's fear, anger, and frustration start to take over. At this level, stress is with the child whether he is awake or asleep.

A bad dream or restless night once in a while are not cause for concern. Even a nightmare on rare occasion is not something about which parents should worry; but if the bad dreams happen often and especially if they are bad enough to call nightmares, the child is experiencing excessive stress.

There are some strategies you can suggest to parents that will comfort their child. First, they should encourage the youngster to have a quiet time before bed. They might talk with him for fifteen or twenty minutes about something positive and not stressful. The idea is to help him slow down and calm down before trying to go to sleep. This slowing down time combined with a regular bedtime helps establish a going to sleep routine that facilitates their child's being relaxed and calm as he falls asleep.

They also should see if sometime during the day they can get him to talk with them about his fears and frustrations. Talking is always the best medicine for stress; but talking specifically about the dreams or nightmares will not help much.

Their conversation could start like this. "Nightmares like the ones you have been having aren't much fun. They usually mean that we're upset or unhappy about something. At least, that's what it's like when I have bad dreams. What's the one thing that's bothering you the most right now?"

Let parents know that nightmares are not uncommon for children three to five-years-old or so and are normally not related to unusual stress. For these children, it is typically enough to help them learn to awaken completely after a bad dream and especially after a nightmare.[7] Also, parents should encourage their child to try to go to the bathroom and always to awaken them when he has a bad dream. Their reassurance while he is still afraid will help. Talking about something to get his mind off the dream often is just the right touch. If things do not get better for school-age children in a couple of weeks or if younger children's nightmares persist and do not gradually reduce, a few counseling sessions are frequently beneficial.

Headaches

Headaches caused by stress and tension are not especially unusual for children but are somewhat more common in teens. Nonetheless, when a child has a headache, it is most likely caused by a minor illness, allergies, undiagnosed vision problems, or getting too hot or tired. If a child has a headache more than once a month or so, it needs assessed by a physician. Of course, if the headache is severe or is accompanied by vomiting, encourage his parents to check with a physician immediately. It is important to rule out possible medical causes before considering stress as a likely cause of their child's headaches.

Trouble with an Upset Stomach

Like headaches, a child's upset stomach is probably caused by something other than stress. It may be from eating too much or eating something that disagreed with him. A minor illness, needing to go to the bathroom, or not feeling well may be the cause. If the discomfort is not severe or continuing, teach parents that rest, a little sympathy, and some personal space are usually right on target.

[7]It is important to emphasize that the child should fully awaken, including gently wiping his face with a damp washcloth, if necessary to get him fully awake. The need is to be sure that the child is clearly separating being awake from being asleep, the bad dream from reality. The parent can calmly say, "Wake up. You are having a bad dream. It is just a dream."

An upset stomach is more likely to be caused by stress than are headaches. When the sign is caused by stress, the child is edgy and afraid of something or someone. Counsel sensitivity. His parents gently encouraging him to talk about what is wrong usually helps a lot.

If talking is not easy for him, this is a good approach for his parents. "I'll bet your stomach is telling us you are afraid or a little uptight about something or someone. Does it have something to do with things here at home, or at school, or maybe with your friends?" If this gets a response, it is important for them to listen, being careful not to pass judgement. Not criticizing the child and not inadvertently implying that his feelings are wrong or unimportant are the keys to supportive listening.

Cries Easily or Has Crying Spells

This sign works much like stomachaches, although the feelings are usually stronger and more confusing for the child. When this sign is observed, offer parents this advice. They should try giving their child a little more space and not push too hard to get him to talk. They want him to know it is okay to sometimes cry and feel upset. They should ask him if he wants to talk about the painful thoughts and feelings. Talking and thinking things through is most always a better alternative for him than crying and his very real pain. Nonetheless, if he does not want to talk, they need to give him a little time and space and then go back quietly to sit for a few minutes and maybe talk. If his crying goes on for more than a couple days, they should try to get him to talk with a counselor at school or with another specialist he trusts.

Loses His Temper Easily and Quickly

This is typically the most difficult sign of stress for parents to handle and the easiest for them to misunderstand. If they are like most adults, they react to the youngster's anger by getting angry. This reaction is followed by trying to stop the child's behavior. With other signs of stress, it is easier to see the child's unhappy feelings and frustration and not so hard to respond to his feelings instead of reacting to his behavior. With temper and anger, parents can find themselves reacting to the child's angry behavior and not responding to his feelings at all.

The best response is difficult but is the soundest advice you can give. His temper outburst will run its course. If he is not hitting someone or breaking things, the outburst does not hurt anything. However his parents respond, they must not get into an argument with him. They need to use all of their adult restraint to avoid yelling or making threats.

Instead, teach them to calmly say, "I can see you're angry. You have a right to feel how you feel. I'm going to wait here with you until you get it out however much you need to blow." Now they need to stop talking and wait until their child starts quieting down and calming down. If the tantrum persists or if they are unable to wait quietly, parents can leave the room for a while, returning when their child is calmer.[8]

When it gets a little quieter, the parents can say, "Being angry is okay sometimes. Losing your temper doesn't work very well for any of us. You're trying very hard to tell me something important. Please try again. When your temper isn't getting in the way, I can hear and understand better. What has you so upset?"

Whatever it is, they should not react, blame their child,[9] give advice, or defend themselves or anyone else. They might say, "Thank you for sharing that with me. I'll think about it and we can talk about it a little later." They need then to be sure to think about it and actually go back later and offer to talk about his frustrations and concerns.

If you encourage parents to consider counseling for their child's stress-related difficulties or for help with other signs of maladjustment, suggest professionals to them who specialize in the specific area of childhood maladjustment about which they are concerned. Not every specialist has expertise with child-related problems; and those who do are not experts in all areas of childhood maladjustment.

If you do not personally know the specialist and are not familiar with his or her qualifications and experience, suggest that the parents talk with the individual by phone before scheduling an appointment. They can ask about his or her training, experience, license status, and treatment philosophy. This also gives the parents an opportunity to see how comfortable they will be with the person who will see their child. You

[8]Some children's tantrums are exacerbated by having someone present. For those youngsters, leaving the room and returning when the child calms is the best approach. For young children, removing the child to another room may be easier. Either he can come back when he is calmer or his parents can go to him to talk about his angry feelings, after he settles.

[9]Trying to find someone to blame is common. Help parents avoid blame-placing whether toward their child, themselves, or someone else. Pointing fingers focuses on finding someone with whom to be angry instead of on the anger itself. It does not help the child more productively experience, express, and manage his anger.

can help them think about appropriate qualifications; but generally, they need to work with a child-specialist who:

- Holds at least one graduate degree in social work, psychology, or mental health-related counseling from an accredited professional program at a reputable university;
- Is a pediatrician or child psychiatrist; or
- Is a State-certified or licensed specialist in another area specifically related to the youngster's difficulty.

In most states, qualified specialists are licensed to practice independently, without supervision by a more qualified practitioner.

CHAPTER 3

DEPRESSION AND SUICIDE

Overview

Children can become so confused about what is going on in their lives and so down on themselves that they can hardly stand it. When the anger, frustration, sense of loss, and confusing feelings that underlie their depression are persistent and not resolved, their depression likely will worsen. They may feel like running away or just giving up on themselves. These are awful, painful feelings. These kids feel afraid, angry, and very upset. They have more stress than they can handle, their self-esteem is very low, and they cannot get their thoughts straightened out or figure out their problems. They believe they have come to the end of their road and see no way out of this lonely place. At the extreme, suicide may seem to them like their only choice.[10] Consider Richard, his depression, and the course his depression might take if no one notices, if no one intervenes.

"What am I doing here? I should've just stayed home. I don't belong here. I don't fit in. I don't fit in anywhere," Richard thinks as he stands by himself watching the party. He wants to join a cluster of young people talking in the kitchen but is afraid. "Even if they let me join in, I'll mess up. I'll just say something dumb or do something stupid and they'll laugh at me. That would be worse than just standing here by myself."

He had told himself he would do better this time. This time he was going to act like he had as much of a right to be there as anyone else. This time he would not just stand around and watch everyone have a good time.

Later that night, Richard is alone in his room. He had left the party after a half hour or so; and no one even noticed.

"No one wants me around. What's wrong with me?" He sits in his chair staring off into space feeling awful. "I knew better. I knew it'd turn out like that. It always does. I was stupid like usual." He feels the tears as he turns off the light and gets into bed. "It's never going to change," he says over and over to himself as he begins quietly sobbing.

---

[10]This chapter discusses signs of depression associated with suicidal feelings and behavior. The signs in the next three chapters may also be associated with depression or have depression as an underlying factor.

Signs of Depression and Suicide

The following questions highlight common signs of depression associated with suicidal feelings and behavior. Parents may mention one or more of them to you and request your advice. Even if parents do not mention any of them, you should explore them anyway to see if their child is exhibiting any of these signs. This will broaden your perspective as you develop the advice you will offer.[11]

As you and the child's parents consider each question, explore whether their child has had the problem within the past month or so. If not, go to the next question. If he has experienced the problem, put a check mark beside the question and then go to the next question. Repeat the process until you have considered each question.

Does their Child:

- Seem not to be getting up and over the loss of an important relationship?
- Seem not to be getting over a serious loss or disappointment?
- Think he cannot do anything about what happens to him?
- Talk about suicide?
- Have a history of attempting suicide?

These are very serious signs and progress from one sign to the next. It is hard for parents to acknowledge that their child has these problems, that their child is depressed and perhaps suicidal. It is easier for them to think he is just having a bad day. Though this may be true, encourage them to think about whether it is just one bad day, whether he has been having a lot of bad days lately. Help them to see if there may be a pattern over a few weeks.

Gently have them consider each sign. Does it apply at all to their child? If so, have them start by assuming that he has the problem. Since it is very easy to dismiss what they see, their safest course is to overinterpret his behavior to be sure they are not taking it too lightly. The following sections will help you better understand signs of depression that can lead to suicidal thoughts and behavior, facilitate parents' pinpointing the key issues, and enable you to appropriately advise them.

---

[11]Although it is uncommon, children under eight-years-old may express suicidal feelings or exhibit suicidal behavior. If so, the dynamics are often different than with older children. If the behavior or feelings persist for more than a few days with younger children, the need for a mental health consultation is urgent. The urgency increases the younger the child.

Not Getting Up and Over the Loss of an Important Relationship

A child's feeling he cannot live without a relationship is his perception of how he would be without the relationship. That is just how it is from his point of view. When parents see this sign in their child, he perceives that the relationship he lost was important, thinks it is gone, and believes he cannot live without it. It does not matter how others see or think about him and the relationship. His perception is his reality and the basis for his actions.

His parents need to start with his reality, with his perceptions. It is easier for them to unilaterally decide that what he thinks and feels is not true, that the relationship was not actually so important, or that he has not really lost the relationship. They say to him, "Things will work out." Their point is that he is wrong.

His parents' helping him starts with adopting his perspective, his perception. Why does he think the relationship was so important? What makes him think he lost the relationship; and most importantly, why does he think he cannot live without it?

Help parents understand that their child will be best served if they start the conversation like this. "I want to understand. Please help me understand. What about the relationship was so important for you? What have you lost that is so very important to you? Will you talk to me about what you're thinking and feeling?"

Their child's grief, anger, fear, and emptiness are real and painful. His loss is real; and living past the pain feels impossible to him. To help, his parents need to share his grief, his strong feelings, and his pain. It is as if they take part of it into themselves. Their child cannot handle it by himself; but between him and his parents, they can.

Here is how they tell if they are helping. Can they feel his loss, his emptiness, his grief, and his pain? Is it a little as if the feelings were theirs? If so, they have achieved empathy. That is the level at which real help and healing can begin.

Of course, encourage the child's parents to refrain from telling him how he should think or feel, and more importantly, from saying that his feelings and how he thinks about what happened are wrong. They need to listen and feel until empathy comes for them. They can then honestly say, "We're afraid for you. We're afraid for us. Maybe we don't totally understand; but we feel awful and hurt as if it happened to us. We want to be close to you and help us get through this. Can we share your grief with you and struggle through it with you?" Holding or touching their child may make him and them feel better; but holding him emotionally is the key to really helping him.

Not Getting Over a Serious Loss or Disappointment

A child's perception is his reality. Anything is disappointing if he feels disappointed. He is the judge. Also, he is the only judge of how disappointing it was for him. This means that not getting invited to a party can be more painful for one child than not getting a college scholarship is for another. Not making the basketball team can devastate one child and not bother another child much one way or the other. It is important for the youngster's parents to listen to what their child is telling them and then believe him. He is the expert on his perceptions.

When a disappointment of any kind is very painful for the youngster, this is what is happening. He had started seeing himself as having what he wanted. In his mind, in the viewfinder of his developing perception, he was someone who had reached his goal. He made the team, was part of the group at the party, was going to be a college student. It matters little what his goal was. It had become part of how he thought about himself, who he thought he was. In his mind, he was a team member, one of the group, someone who fit in, who belonged. It is how children think about and understand important things.

The child's loss may be because of embarrassment and humiliation, because a relationship is no longer there for him, because of a severe disappointment. Whatever its cause, it is less belonging for him. He can come to believe that he does not belong at all, anywhere.

Teach the child's parents to say, "I know a lot about disappointment. I think you may even know more than I do right now. I remember how awful and painful it feels. I remember it feels like a huge crash or sometimes like suddenly losing everything important. Can we talk about how you're feeling? What's the first thing that comes to your mind?" Their objective is, of course, to get him to talk about his disappointment, about his loss. At the same time, though, they need to encourage him to talk about his feelings, especially his angry feelings.

Another example will help to show how disappointment, loss of status, and feeling embarrassed and not accepted can lead to depression and suicidal feelings. It also shows how events can accumulate and compound.

Things are going from bad to worse for Holly. It starts when her brother dies in a car wreck. He was her best buddy, when they were not arguing. Steve was the only person in her life she could talk with about things that really mattered. Steve just listened and thought she was pretty.

She knows she will never get over Steve's leaving her but can handle that and maybe even the stuff with her stepfather. At least she does not have to worry about dealing with him every day now since she and her mother have moved away.

Things are getting worse, though. She finally gets up her nerve to try out for cheerleading and now wishes she never had to go to school again. She thought it might be different in this school. "I should've left well enough alone. It doesn't get you many friends; but being the best math student in the school should've been enough." She can hardly stop shaking inside when she thinks about "the incident," which is only a thousand times a day.

The competition is in front of everyone at a pep rally. It starts out well enough until it is Holly's turn. Not only does she forget the words to the cheer, she falls into the pep band while trying to make a jump. If hurting herself is not enough, she also feels like the joke of the school.

But just when she knows it cannot get any worse, it does. A new boy in school moves in on her one special place. Not only is he a math whiz, everyone likes him, including the math teacher. Her teacher's saying, "Being the second best math student in the school is nothing to feel badly about," only makes her feel worse.

"There's nothing special about me anymore. At least Steve thought I was pretty and now he is dead. It's all too much."

Holly's world is out of control. "Being dead would be a relief. There is no way out. I can't stand this. I've got to do something to stop the pain. I just want out."

Thinks He Cannot Do Anything About What Happens to Him

This sign is the can hardly live without it, the cannot face it, the not getting over it, the cannot handle it part of the other signs. It is the child's feeling of having lost control within his life and being unable to get control back.[12] Just as belonging is important to him, so is believing he is in control of what happens to him. At least, he needs to know his life is not out of control.

The child feels very little control and thinks he does not belong, does not fit in. This is what is causing his bad, painful feelings.

His anger is a very bad feeling he has about what happened to him; and his fear is a very bad feeling he has about what he believes will

---

[12]Children need power, control, and influence: power to cause things to happen within their worlds, control over what happens to them, and the ability to influence the important people in their lives to accept them, meet their needs, and respond to their interests. All three are necessary for children to "make a difference."

happen. He is angry about the position he is now in and about his future having been changed. Things are just not working out as they should, from his point of view. His fear is a little less complicated. Who knows what might happen? Even worse, he knows, is sure what will happen and it scares him.

The child either did not or could not control what happened and is very angry. He cannot control what he believes will happen and is afraid. The less control he feels, the more angry and afraid he gets and the more hopeless he feels. It is a building pressure.

It is important to help him get these feelings out. This holds most for his anger, as discussed earlier. Additionally, there is another important step.

The child's parents should give him as much power and control as they can. They need to let him handle things with their support whenever they can. Encourage them to refrain from telling him what to do or how to act. Of course they should talk with him about these things but also should let him be in charge of himself and his actions as much as possible.

Young people's parents usually cannot do much about the big things that get out of control for them; but it really is the little things that count. For all children but especially for older youngsters, parents need to let them have as much control as possible over as much as possible. As odd as it may seem at first, this may be parents' single best way to help their children handle their anger and fear.[13]

Talks About Suicide

Suicidal thoughts and feelings build in children. Anger and fear fester, negative perceptions and strong emotions accumulate, and the child's perceived lack of control grows. This building internal turmoil creates intense negative energy that boils up until suicide becomes an attractive solution. It starts as a possibility and slowly becomes the child's first choice.

The young person thinks about suicide more and more. He considers it and then rejects the idea. Finally, he reconsiders it, struggles to find other answers, and comes back to suicide as the only relief from his

---

[13]Parents should talk with their children about letting them have as much control as possible. They can talk and plan together about activities, decisions, and other areas in which the youngsters want and can have more control and some areas in which they may be able to handle complete control. Parents must then remember that "a deal is a deal."

anger, fear, pain, his emptiness. It becomes his final way of assuming power, of taking control of his world.

About 80 percent of the time, children will tell someone about their thoughts and talk about their solution. If they are believed, whomever they tell can and usually does get help for them. Far too often, though, no one takes the child's talking about suicide seriously.

Children do not normally say things like, "I wish I were dead," "I would be better off dead," or "I think I will just kill myself." It is not true youngsters often say those kinds of things or are just joking around when they say them. If someone asks them about it, they often do say they were not serious and were just joking around. They may be embarrassed, may want to hide their real feelings, or may not be comfortable talking about suicide with whomever is present. Still, it is no joking matter and they likely were not just joking.

The child may bring up suicide in a joking way or may bring it up in a serious way. He may seem quite depressed or may seem fairly normal for him. Whatever his mood, the need is to respond to what he is saying. If his parents are talking with him, suggest that they ask, "What are you thinking about doing? It feels to me like you may be thinking about killing yourself. Am I on track or off base?" Their child may spontaneously start talking about suicide, someone who killed himself, or ways to kill oneself. However he discloses his thoughts, the opportunity to help is right then.

If he says that he was just kidding, teach his parents to say, "Let's think about some better ways to get your feelings out. When you joke about killing yourself, what's your message? I'll bet it has something to do with feeling upset, something to do with feeling angry and maybe a little afraid and a lot to do with feeling hopeless. Let's talk about it if you will. What are you thinking and feeling when you joke about killing yourself?"

Talking about suicide helps. It neither makes things worse nor makes it more likely the young person will kill himself. His parents can say, "I'm afraid for you. I'm afraid for both of us. Can we talk about what's happening?"

It is, of course, possible that their child is threatening suicide to get his parents' attention but not very likely. Even if he is seeking their attention, he can back himself into a corner if he keeps it up. He says it so much that everyone stops taking him seriously. He has to take it one step further if only to save face. The next step for him is actually trying to kill himself; and he might just succeed, even if only by accident.

Without a doubt, it was very serious the first time he threatened. If he is dead, whether he was serious or just wanting attention no longer matters. His parents will not get another chance to take him seriously.

What is going on with a child who uses threats of suicide to get attention? There are many possibilities, none of which is good. Teach the youngster's parents to say, "A part of me believes you want to kill yourself and the other part thinks you are using threatening suicide to get my attention. Either way, I'm very concerned. Can we talk about the getting attention side?" The conversation goes on for a little while and they then say, "Threatening is an effective way to get attention. You certainly got mine. It worked. Here's my problem. When you use suicide to get my attention, it scares me and is a little frustrating. I like to pay attention to you so you don't have to scare me to get my attention. It's yours. I have some ideas but want to hear your ideas first. What are some other ways you could let me know when you want my attention, want me to take you more seriously, want me to understand how bad it is for you?"

You and they also might spend some time thinking about why getting their attention is so difficult for their child. That likely will point toward other problems.

Be sure parents keep this focus. Suicidal thoughts and feelings are always serious. The youngster needs specialized help immediately, in addition to his parents' support, involvement, and sensitivity. Further, be sure his parents understand that the crisis has not passed as soon as their child's thoughts turn to other subjects or as soon as his mood brightens. Among many needs, the child must develop better ways of communicating his feelings, solving his problems, and getting others to understand and help. The underlying distress continues past the here-and-now symptoms.[14]

Suicide Attempts

Most children who kill themselves have attempted suicide before. Also, many children who attempt suicide will later kill themselves. The point is that a suicide attempt is always serious no matter how trivial it may seem at the time and no matter how non-lethal the means used. It is

[14]It is unfortunately not always possible to tell that a child is or may be suicidal. As much as a third of the time, there were no signs or symptoms exhibited that could have predicted suicide.

not necessarily true that the child knew that the method he used would not kill him.[15]

Suicide is a process and not a single act. It is seldom just something that happened. The child thinks about it for a long time. He adds up his losses, disappointments, humiliations, times he does not fit in, and when he thinks he does not belong. These all build up to feelings of not being in control, hopelessness, and being unable to make things better. A child who attempts suicide always needs counseling and special help to understand these intense feelings and to learn new ways to manage them. He also needs his parents, needs to talk with them about his fears and frustrations, his anger and emptiness.[16]

---

[15]The non-lethality of the means is occasionally used by adults (including parents, school personnel, and others) as "proof" that the child was not serious. This rationalization is frequently a form of denial, a means of hiding embarrassment, and a subconscious way of avoiding dealing with the child's having tried to kill himself.

[16]You will find it useful to read Crow, Gary A. and Crow, Letha I., *Crisis Intervention And Suicide Prevention: Working with Children and Adolescents.* Charles C Thomas, Springfield, IL, 1987.

CHAPTER 4

LEARNING PROBLEMS

Overview

Children who are doing very well in school are proportionally about the same as those who are having serious problems. Generally, about 20 percent of children are very successful in school and about 20 percent are in serious trouble academically or because of behavior problems. The other 60 percent or so are somewhere in between. Most children are in this middle group where they may need help but their problems are not pervasive or at a crisis level.

What about the 20 percent at the top? Check back in twenty or thirty years. Most of them will be teachers, doctors, scientists, business people and leaders in the community. In short, they will continue to succeed.

What about the 20 percent at the bottom? It is sad but true that most of them will still be at the bottom. Some will succeed but most will not. It is easy to spot these kids when they are teenagers dropping out of school or getting into trouble with the police and headed nowhere. These high-risk children are harder to spot when they are five and six and seven. Nonetheless, they are alive and failing today.

Advising parents about school and learning problems their children are having starts with their seeing that learning is not simple. There are three important areas they need to consider. First, their child's abilities are fundamental to his learning. Some children learn easier than others. However easily their child learns, he learns some things more easily than others. Some assignments and subjects are easier for him and others are more difficult. Even if he is a very good learner, learning is hard work at times.

Next, his attitude is important. Does he want to learn? Is he willing to do what he needs to do to get the job done? It comes down to this. Does he think he is important enough to work at it? Is his future important enough to him to bother learning? Learning takes self-discipline and hard work. It also takes an attitude that says, "I'm important enough to do what I have to do."

Third, their child needs to develop learning skills. Some of these skills help him pay attention and study, some help him listen and try to understand, and some help him cooperate and follow the rules. He also learns about what adults expect and about the rights of others. If their child has problems learning, encourage his parents to look at his abilities, attitudes, and skills.

To start the process of helping parents think about their child's learning success and school adjustment, discuss these three questions with them. First, does their child have the ability to do assigned school work? It is easy and natural for parents to answer yes to the question. No one likes thinking his child does not have the ability to succeed; but unfortunately, some youngsters do not. Here is how parents can tell.

If their child does well with some assignments, he likely has the ability to do the work. If they have not seen him do well on a repeated basis, they do not know whether he has the ability.

They can start their evaluation by talking to their child's teacher. If she says he has the ability, they should have her show them several examples of his work where he did well. If she cannot do this, they and she need to check into it further. Most teachers know how to do this and have access to the necessary resources through the school.[17]

If a specific child's teacher either cannot or will not pursue the needed information and resources, the youngster's parents should talk directly with the school's principal, psychologist, or counselor. If this does not move the process along, you can refer them to a specialist in the community who will work with the child and his parents and who will advocate for him within his school.

Next, have his parents evaluate their child's attitude. Is he generally positive about school and learning? If not, there is a problem. It may have to do with his confidence and self-esteem. It also may be because he is not very successful at school. Counsel parents to remember this. Bad attitudes are much more likely caused by failure than is failure caused by a bad attitude. Failure and little to no success come first. The bad

---

[17]Be sure that parents do not accept an explanation that starts with, "Your child could do well if he wanted to; but he does not because he does not try hard enough." Explanations that start with blaming the child are ill-considered and are unlikely to lead to performance improvement.

attitude comes last. Unfortunately, the bad attitude is what many parents tend to notice first and are most likely to see as the problem.

Finally, does their child have the skills he needs to succeed? If he is not succeeding, this is the most likely source of his difficulties. It is unusual to see a child who knows how to succeed but fails anyway. It happens but is a most uncommon kind of learning and school adjustment problem. Their child's having this problem is very unlikely; and he deserves his parents' sincere effort to find out what the real issues are.

Once in a while, you will talk with parents who are totally blaming their child's difficulties on teachers or other school personnel. They are unwilling to consider the possibility that his difficulties may have more to do with his personal issues than with people at school. Although their explanation may be valid, it is very unlikely. Even if there is a large measure of truth in it, their intransigently taking that position with the school is unlikely to help their child much. If you are talking with parents who are using the "It's the school's fault," approach, suggest this.

Have them talk with their child's teacher or the school's principal. They should start the conversation like this. "I'm very concerned about my child's lack of success at school. He's having a lot of trouble relating to people and learning what he needs to learn. It's hard for me to say quite what accounts for his problems. It looks to me like he isn't getting a fair shake; but I'm his parent and may not be completely objective. Whatever the cause, I want to see him succeed, as I know you do too. I'm wondering if we could come up with a couple of things we and he could work on; or perhaps we could identify a specialist who could help us work this out. Either way, he deserves our cooperative efforts. What do you think? What do you think is our best strategy?" Most always, this approach moves the process in a positive direction.

Signs of Learning and School Difficulty

You have helped the parents see that their child's ability, attitude, and skills combine to determine whether he will succeed in school. Now, have them consider some common signs of learning and school difficulties. Through this activity, they will learn how to evaluate how well their child is doing and what types of problems he may be having. You can then look with them at each of these signs in more detail and consider how they can best help him.

Think with the child's parents about the following questions. They get at common signs of learning and school problems. Consider each question, asking the parents if their child ever has the problem. If not, go to the next question. If he sometimes has the problem, put a check mark beside the question and then go to the next question. Repeat the process until his parents have thought about each question.

Does Their Child:

- Have problems understanding school assignments and what teachers expect?
- Have trouble understanding what he reads?
- Get confused about what he is doing, what people expect, or what people are saying?
- Find that trying harder does not lead to his homework and other assignments getting better and easier?
- Do some assignments very well and others very badly?
- Forget to do homework or have trouble remembering what was assigned?
- Have difficulty following instructions and directions?
- Have a problem paying attention to time or managing time?
- Get bad grades?
- Have trouble asking for help or letting anyone help?
- Have difficulty accepting or dealing with criticism?
- Always have excuses for not doing well?
- Think his not doing well is someone else's fault?
- Have to have an adult standing over him to get him to do his school work?
- Feel teachers and other adults at school have it in for him?
- Disrupt the classroom or the activities of other children?
- Make no effort to cooperate and get along?
- Skip school or miss school a lot?

Did you or his parents spot any problems? If not, the child is likely doing quite well in school. His parents should be pleased with him and also pleased with themselves. Their hard work and efforts are paying off nicely for both their child and them.

It is more likely that signs of difficulty were identified. Most children have some school and learning issues that need attention. If you or the youngster's parents have identified potential problems, reconsider those questions. Put a 1, 2 or 3 next to the question. A "1" means his parents see the problem once in a great while. For those problems, have the parents talk with their child about their concern and then watch for a couple weeks to see if things get better. They usually do.

Put a "2" beside the question if the problem has been noticed more than once a month. For those problems, have the parents talk with the child about their concern and also mention it to his teacher. If they cannot stop by school, they should call her at school or in the evening. The school office will either give them her number or have her call the parents at a time that is convenient for them. Teachers normally want to hear from parents. If they cannot get in touch with the teacher, they should feel comfortable calling the principal at the child's school. They should then follow any suggestions they get from the school's professional staff. If they are uncomfortable doing this, encourage them to discuss the advice they received with you so you can help them understand it better. If necessary, you can then talk with the people at school to get their ideas firsthand. This may help you more appropriately advise the parents.

Put a "3" beside any question that identifies a problem that the parents have seen once a week or more. Something is certainly wrong, and the parents need to talk with the child's teacher as soon as they can. Help them understand that something more is happening than will be fixed by simply telling their child to pay more attention, listen better, study more, or work harder. All of these are ways of blaming their child for having the problem. He needs to take his share of responsibility for things getting better; but his parents, with the assistance of the people at school, need to do their share of the work too. It will take all of them to help him. It is not just his problem, and each of them must take responsibility for understanding and working on the child's difficulties.

Problems Understanding School Assignments and What Teachers Expect

The most likely reason for this is easy for parents to miss. It is because the assignment or expectation was not clear. This is usually the trouble if the problem comes up mostly with one teacher or with another specific adult. If the problem comes up with several people, however, something else is likely going on.

Be sure parents put vision and hearing problems at the top of their list of possible explanations. Although undetected vision and hearing problems are uncommon with schoolage children, the possibility must not be overlooked. It is important to make the point with parents that whispering and talking quietly do not adequately test their child's hearing and that simply looking at objects or pictures does not adequately test his vision. If he has not been seen by an optometrist specializing in children's vision within the last year, a vision examination should always be done when trying to understand learning related problems. An evaluation by an audiologist is necessary only if the child's teacher, school nurse, psychologist, or pediatrician recommends it. It is nonetheless important to ask one or more of these specialists whether the child may have a hearing problem and need a specialized evaluation.

Once vision and hearing problems have been eliminated as underlying causes, attention can turn to other possibilities. For example, perhaps he did not understand because he was not paying attention. This could be because he did not think the assignment was interesting or important, or maybe he figured he would mess it up anyway.

Children with low self-esteem often think there is little point in trying. Sometimes these kids find themselves in a vicious circle. They think they cannot do anything, so they do not try. Since they do not try, they fail, and their lack of success reinforces the belief that they cannot do anything. The circle is complete, and the youngsters are caught in a self-fulfilling prophecy: "I can't, therefore I don't, therefore I fail, which proves I can't."

Two other possibilities need some attention. He might have special problems paying attention. For example, he might have Attention Deficit Hyperactivity Disorder (ADHD). Be sure the child is seen by a child psychologist or by a pediatrician to evaluate this possibility if he consistently has trouble paying attention. These specialists will check for other possible problems at the same time.

The other possibility is harder to assess. The assignment or what the teacher expects may be beyond the child's learning and experience. He has not learned what he needs to know to understand the assignment. This may be because his education has been neglected, because of serious mental or emotional problems, or because the child does not have the needed ability. Parents may not want to accept these as possibilities but the child deserves consideration of every possible explanation.

The child's not understanding can be complicated. His parents need to keep an open mind as well as continue to encourage and support him while they explore possible explanations. The key to their support is not to do anything he may read as blaming him. It is not his fault he does not understand. There likely is more to it than his simply being difficult and not cooperating.

Trouble Understanding What He Reads

A child's not understanding what he reads is a serious problem. In fact, it may be the single most important sign of learning and school problems and can have several causes.

Vision problems go at the top of the list; but as mentioned earlier, undiscovered vision problems are fairly unlikely. More likely are illness, difficulty concentrating and paying attention, not liking what is available to read, or finding the effort required a bit much. Whatever the cause, not understanding what he reads usually has little to nothing to do with things like not trying, being lazy, or a bad attitude. These kinds of things could cause a child not to read; but they would have nothing to do with understanding or not understanding. When this sign is present, the child goes through the motions of reading. It just does not lead to understanding.

If his parents ask him to read a page from one of his school books and he looks at all the words, he has gone through the motions of reading. They then ask a question or two and discover that he does not understand. What is happening?

The possibilities include his not being smart enough to understand, not knowing some of the new words, or not knowing anything about the ideas or subject area. Any of these problems could cause him to have trouble understanding and should be assessed. The problem usually has little to do with these kinds of things. It is more likely he has a reading disability.

There are several kinds of reading disabilities. Most commonly, they involve perception: the child sees what is on the page but has trouble making any sense of the marks and squiggles. He may see things backward or upside down, may be unable to track the line of print across the page, or may have problems keeping oriented on the page. A reading specialist[18] can help define the problem(s) and suggest ways to help him. If available, a school psychologist is the best resource for this evaluation.

Keep this point in mind as you work with parents. Children who can

---

[18]Most schools have a teacher who specializes in reading-related problems. Also, many communities have private learning centers for children who are having difficulties. If a private service is considered, advise parents to consult with their child's school and with other parents whose children have been served by the service before enrolling their child.

learn usually do learn. Youngsters who can read and understand usually do. When a child has a problem with reading or in other learning areas, merely trying harder is very unlikely to do any good.

Gets Confused About What He Is Doing, What People Expect or What People Are Saying

Parents will notice this sign in their child in a couple ways. First, he may have trouble getting the story straight when talking about things that happened. He might leave out important details, get things out of order, not have the time element right, or misread the motives or behavior of people.

The problem also can come up in a different way. Their child gets into trouble. He is surprised, does not understand, and may become angry, very upset, and then get into more trouble. It is like a confusing snowball. When it gets as big as it is going to get, the child has no idea what happened. He just figures he is in trouble again for who knows why. It is for sure he does not know.

This sign can cause the child to have problems at home and can cause him to have behavior problems at school. He also is likely to have other school problems because he gets as confused in class as he does most everywhere he goes. Many children who have trouble getting along have this problem.

This kind of difficulty is hard to diagnose and understand. The child may have more problems in some situations than in others. It is hard to predict. It also can spill over into what he reads. He may get as confused about events in a book as in the real world.

The parents' first step is to accept the problem when it is there. There are many other explanations that are quicker and easier. It is easier to chalk the problem up to not paying attention, lying, not trying, and on and on. Youngsters do get confused; and for some, it is a serious learning problem. An example may help.

> Jerry is fifteen and is suspended from school. The latest mess goes like this. He has been doing well for almost three months which is a long time for Jerry. It starts one Thursday when he gets into it with a teacher.
>
> "She just cracked on me and gave me a detention."
>
> He is asked why she did this. "I don't know. She doesn't like kids. She likes all the power. I wasn't doing anything. She just comes up and tells me I have to move."

He is asked why she wanted him to move. "Who knows? She just likes jerking kids around."

A few minutes later, he goes on, "I don't have to take it from her and told her so."

He is asked what happened then. "I'm suspended, aren't I? What does it look like happened?"

No, he is not covering up; he really does not understand what happened. Whenever a child has difficulties at school, gets into trouble, or messes something up, he may be getting confused. It is a serious problem and deserves the same attention as would be given to any other learning disability.[19]

Trying Harder Does Not Lead to His Homework and Other Assignments Getting Better and Easier

This sign is very common for children with learning problems. If it goes unnoticed, and it often does, they finally get to where they just quit trying. Have parents whose children exhibit this sign think about this. Suppose they (the parents) had tried for years to learn how to do something and could not learn to do it. Add to this people who keep telling them, "You aren't trying hard enough." "You just need to put forth more effort." "You're failing, and some day you'll wish you had taken advantage of the opportunity." How long do they think they would keep trying? What would their attitude be? How would they react to those people? Maybe they are saints; but if they are like most of us, they would probably do and say things that should not be put in writing here.

It may be that the youngsters who dig in and fight back are the healthy ones. The ones who passively keep trying may have another kind of problem. Whatever parents think they would do, help them see that trying harder and still not succeeding is extraordinarily frustrating for their child.

What is wrong? Why is their child not learning, not succeeding? For his sake, they need to find the answers before he joins the ranks of those who just quit.

With some exceptions, children who do not do well in school are trying as hard as those who are doing well, those for whom school comes

[19]You may want to consider "Social Intelligence" or "EQ." The idea is that there is a body of knowledge about people and social skills that some children master more completely and easily than others. One implication is that parents may need to explicitly teach their children social ideas and concepts they may have assumed they already knew.

easier. It does not take as long to do homework if the child knows how to do it. It does not take as much effort to read assignments if he is a good reader. "It isn't fair. I spent two hours to get a D and others spent less than an hour to get B's. I quit!" Anytime their child is not learning, his parents need to help him find out why. It likely has little to do with anything that will improve by his simply trying harder.

Does Some Assignments Very Well and Others Very Badly

This sign can be hard to spot since it goes against the way most parents think about learning and achievement. Any child might have a bad day, get a bad grade, or just not do very well. This sign gets at something a little different, though.

Youngsters' performance and achievement are normally fairly consistent over time and across the board. If a child gets A's and B's in some subjects, it is unusual for him to get D's and F's in other subjects. Here, we are talking about basic subjects such as Science, English, History, Math, Social Studies, and the like. Subjects such as Music, Physical Education, and Shop sometimes do not show the same pattern, although they usually do. Getting D's and F's typically does not go with getting A's and B's. If the pattern for a child is not consistent, there is often a problem needing attention. Consider this example!

> Renee is in the seventh grade and is a good student. This year, she is failing math. She is told that she is not paying attention, not trying hard enough, and that Math is just harder for girls. The message is that it is her fault.
>
> Her parents do not accept these explanations and look for other reasons. As it turns out, there are three problems. First, she is now in middle school and is a little intimidated. The work includes some beginning Algebra and she is afraid to ask her teacher for extra help. Next, she has a habit of being a little sloppy and is not keeping numbers and other symbols aligned on her paper. This is causing her to become confused. Finally, she believes boys are better at math than girls and thinks she is just not a good math student. The result is failure.
>
> With a little extra help and support from her parents including some additional attention to neatness, her math grades go up to B's.

There may be many reasons for this problem. Some subjects emphasize reading more while others emphasize thinking and discussion, some are more visual and others are more mental, some add to knowledge and skills the child already has while others add new ideas, involve new applications, and require new skills. When parents see a big difference in how their child does from one subject to another, they need to work with him to figure out why. The underlying problem is likely not his fault.

This sign also comes up with activities away from school. How well youngsters do most day-to-day things is usually consistent from activity to activity. Parents should be concerned if their child normally does average or above in most things and has a few things he does badly.

Help them consider this question. What do the activities where he has trouble have in common? The child's difficulties likely have something to do with one or more of the common elements. It might be eye-hand coordination, working in groups, getting organized, or something else.

If they watch closely and give some thought to it, the problem can usually be identified. This gives them a chance to give their child some extra help and an opportunity to point him toward activities where the problem does not get in the way so much. They want him to spend most of his time doing what he does well, understanding that he needs success as much as he needs to improve his skills.

Forgets to Do Homework or Has Trouble Remembering What Was Assigned

Real memory problems are uncommon; but forgetting or not remembering to remember is very common. If it only happens once in a while and seldom involves important things, it is not especially important. It is a problem, though, if forgetting is a regular reason for not doing things. It does get to a point when "I forgot," is not just one of those things.

It may be tempting for parents to accuse their child of lying or not paying attention; and either may be true. If so, they are themselves problems needing the parents' careful attention; but several other explanations are more likely.

First, their child did not see the assignment or expectation as important enough to remember. He thought it did not matter that much. Dealing with this is not complicated and is a good place for parents to start when they first notice the sign. They can talk with him about how important they think the assignment or expectation is and stress with him how necessary they think it is for him to treat it as important. This often helps a lot all by itself.

In addition, parents can help their child to use memory prompts. For example, keeping an assignment notebook can serve to jog the youngster's memory. Also, a list of things the child needs to do will serve to remind him. Posting a family calendar on the refrigerator with notes about chores, appointments, and when assignments are due may help. If these kinds of prompts are used, a small reward for remembering to keep the notebook or look at the list or calendar will reinforce the child's remembering.

Also, they need to be sure that they are not using "I forgot," with him or others in the family over things they were responsible for or had agreed to do. Remembering is a part of caring, respecting each other, and living in a family.

The next step for parents is to be sure their child understands what they expect of him. When they ask him to do something, they might have him repeat their request and briefly tell them how he will go about doing whatever it was.

They can take five minutes for him to explain his homework assignments and describe to them how he will do them. He might tell them, for example, "I'll start on page 144 and read to the end of page 147. I'll work the nine problems on page 201, too." The point is for them to be sure he knows what to do before they expect him to remember to do it.

The next step, if the first ones do not work, is to set some clear consequences for not remembering. They might say, "You forget to do your homework a lot. I also know you often forget to clean your room. You say they are important but you don't act like they are. I want to make them a little more important. Here's how I'm going to do it. We'll work on organizing and scheduling things. You and I are then going to figure out what'll happen each time you forget to do your homework or clean your room. There need to be consequences. What should they be? If we can't decide together, I'll decide for us. What do you think?"

When they use a negative consequence, caution them to be careful. It needs to be mild. The point is to help the child remember and not to punish him for forgetting. It also needs to be something they can do daily if necessary and something they will remember. Their forgetting would itself be a problem.

Since it comes up occasionally, be sure parents do not use this approach. Their child is having difficulties in school or "forgets" to do homework or complete other tasks. As they work with him, they get increasingly frustrated. Mostly out of their frustration, they begin to escalate the negative consequences. For example, they "ground" him for one day to make their point. He does not immediately comply; and they escalate the grounding to two days, and then three days, and then a week. Eventually, they restrict him from more and more activities and make him quit the baseball team and on and on. Instead of things getting better, they go from bad to worse.

These parents do not understand that children seldom learn things the first time, including better work habits and more acceptable patterns of behavior. The approach they should have used is to set the negative consequence and stick to it. If being grounded for one day is the consequence, they should impose that consequence each time, as many times as necessary. Also, the consequence should not be additive. One day's problems should not lead to more than one day's grounding. The key for the parents is consistency and persistence, not escalation.

Difficulty Following Instructions and Directions

This sign typically is because the child did not understand the direction or just forgot. It likely does not have much to do with defiance or intentionally not cooperating. His parents need first to be sure he heard the instruction or has read the direction. They should have him repeat it to them and tell them how he will follow it. This lets them know that he heard the instruction and understood it.

They might say, "Change your clothes after school." When their child tells them how he will do it, some detail is important. When he gets home, what are the steps?

- He goes to his room.
- He takes off his school clothes.
- He gets out his after-school clothes and puts his school clothes where they belong.
- He then gets dressed and goes onto his next activity. Most any instruction can be put into a series of steps to follow. Also, the earlier discussion on forgetting works here too.

Problems Paying Attention to Time or Managing Time

This is a complicated sign. It has as much to do with the example parents set for their child as anything. Their setting a good example will help as will letting him know that they think time is important.

Be sure they can answer *Yes* to these questions before pressing their child to manage his time better.

- Are they usually on time?
- Do things happen at regular times such as dinner time?

- Do they usually get everything done that they planned for the day?
- When they tell him it will be a few minutes, does it actually happen in a few minutes?
- Are they setting a good example?

Discuss these additional points with the child's parents. Doing his school work has a lot to do with time management. Their child needs to get to school on time and get to class on time after he gets to school. He needs to do school work in the time he is given to do it and then turn it in on time. He needs to figure out how long work will take and pace himself so he gets it done.

The child's time management problems usually are because of several things. Not seeing how long projects and activities will take is the most common. Getting better at this requires thinking about it, making estimates and seeing how they work out, and remembering how long it took the last time. Another common problem is not keeping at it. Putting off starting, getting distracted, daydreaming, quitting before finishing, and other bad habits get in the way.

This sign may be due to a more general learning problem, but it usually is not. Normally, it has mostly to do with bad work habits and not staying on task.

Gets Bad Grades

A bad grade once in a great while is not particularly significant. Even the reason for it is not all that important if it only happens very occasionally. This point applies to things like a single day's homework, a specific test, or individual assignments. It does not apply to grade cards or to whole subjects. They represent many grades over time. If a child gets a D or F on his grade card or frequently gets bad grades in a specific subject, he has a problem.

Think with his parents about this. What is a bad grade? It is not unusual to hear someone say, "He could get A's if he wanted to." Here is the fact. Youngsters who can get A's by making a reasonable effort get A's. It is as simple as that. If he does not get A's, either he really cannot or it would take a superhuman effort. Some extra effort is good; but if it goes too far, the good grade comes at the expense of other activities and at a very high cost in stress and pressure. The A is not worth it. Perfection can be given far too much importance.

C's are average in most schools. Average children get mostly C's. If he is getting mostly C's or a C among the B's, his parents should let him know that they think he is doing fine. A little pep talk to get him to hang in there and give it his best is okay too. Any more pressure than this is a bad idea. It can actually make things worse.

Bad grades are D's and F's. If a child is getting bad grades in one or two subjects or in most subjects, there is a serious problem.

First, the child's parents should suspect a reading problem. There usually is one. Next, help them consider the full range of possible learning problems. They need to keep looking until an answer is found. When they see this sign, it is unlikely it is the youngster's fault or that he can do anything about it by himself. If someone advises them that he just needs to try harder, they need to find someone else who better understands learning and children. You can help them identify a specialist who can help them and their child figure out what is wrong.

Trouble Asking for Help or Letting Anyone Help

The life experiences of some children have taught them that asking for help is a bad idea. When they asked for assistance, it was not forthcoming, or perhaps it was offered but was either not helpful or was unpleasant for them. For example, "You should already know." "You'd have known this if you'd listened and paid attention." "I'm tired of your bothering me."

These youngsters also may see asking for help as a sign of weakness or failure. This is not unusual for children whose self-esteem is low. A good starting point is for parents to ask themselves if they have supportively helped when their child asked for help.

Too much help is sometimes a problem too. It can work like this.

The child asks, "Will you show me how to work this problem?"

His parents respond, "This is a good time to get into the ideas and concepts associated with math. Let's start back a few pages to see if you have everything up to this point."

When parents try to help, especially with school work, they often give more help and take much more time than their child had in mind. He may want some help but may not want to spend an hour and sit through a lecture to get it.

For some children, the problem is not knowing how and when to ask for help. If they ask, they do not know how to accept and use the help they get.

Here are some tips you can share with parents:

- Let him know that they are interested.
- Ask what he is studying, what he did in school today, what he thinks about what he did at school.
- Ask him to tell them about what he reads.
- Ask him to show them how to work a math problem or what the point of an experiment is.
- Get into the habit of talking with him about his school work.

If their child is having a problem, teach parents to say, "You're having trouble with that. If you want, I'll help you with it some time." They should not insist on helping him right then. If he has not asked for their help in a day or two, they should ask, "Did you figure out how to do the assignment we were talking about?" If he says he has, they need to follow up with a question or two to be sure. If he has not, they need to ask what his plan is to learn what he needs to learn.

Be sure that the parents keep this caution in mind. They should only give as much help as he wants and can accept. If he misspells a word and asks for help, they should usually just tell him how to spell it. Dictionary lessons can come later. He asks how to work a math problem. They can simply work the problem while he watches.

Have them start by giving him the help he wants in the way he wants it. As time goes on, it will get easier for him to ask for and use their assistance.

Two other groups of youngsters have a somewhat different problem asking for and accepting help. They are children who are either too into being perfect or are unusually strong-willed. As parents try to manage these kids, the problem often is the young people's negative or angry reactions. They get upset and let anyone and everyone know that they want no part of what is being offered.

Their parents can push them just a little; but help the parents understand that a fight is not good. Suggest that they say, "Your angry reaction to my trying to help you is a problem. I'm going to hang in there with you and try to help anyway. If you want to react so badly, go for it. Learning to accept a little help is about as important for you as what you need help with." Support the parents in remembering that their success will come through trying to help and then trying again. Helping their child is a slow process and not a reason to go to war.

Difficulty Accepting or Dealing with Criticism

If a youngster can constructively handle criticism, he can manage almost any problem, including most learning problems. If not, helping him is difficult and can be quite tedious. Have his parents start by talking with their child about the problem. Their goal should be to understand how criticism feels to him, to sense what he thinks and feels when someone criticizes him. Until they and he get past the problem, it will be hard to help, hard to deal with anything.

This is the bind. Their talking with him about the problem is itself criticism. They are criticizing how he handles criticism. Suggest this approach. "You have me in a real bind. I have experience and know some good stuff. I learned most of it by doing things wrong and making mistakes. Here's my problem. Sometimes I see you learning the way I did. I see you are doing something wrong or in a way that doesn't work very well. I think it would be easier for you if I told you what I'd learned; but when I do, you get upset or bent out of shape. That makes me feel like 'Why bother?' Should I say something or just let you learn the hard way?"

Always Has Excuses for Not Doing Well

When children always have excuses for not doing well, the excuses are usually exactly what accounts for the problem. They say that they did not know what to do, did not understand, forgot to do their work, thought they had done it right, did not hear, and on and on. After a while, their excuses wear thin. It is easy for parents to get frustrated and react negatively; but a better reaction is for them to take their child at his word. It is probably the truth.

Encourage parents to use this approach. They can first listen to their child's excuse and then say, "I believe you. What you told me is exactly what happened. I also want you to learn the difference between an excuse and a reason. A reason is an explanation. An excuse makes it sound like it was okay. Your not doing well isn't okay. Now that we understand the reason, we're going to figure out a way to keep it from happening. You say you didn't do well because you didn't hear the assignment. Let's talk about how to be sure you hear and understand assignments."

Be sure the parents are staying calm and focused on the reason. It is a problem to solve and not an excuse for them to blame their child.

Thinks His Not Doing Well Is Someone Else's Fault

This sign is an example of the last sign. Thinking it was someone else's fault is an excuse. After talking about the difference between excuses and reasons, teach parents to say, "You think the reason you didn't do well is your teacher's fault. Tell me how it is her fault. That's a good problem for us to work on."

In another situation, they might say, "Let me see if I understand. Your friend, Joe, mouthed off to you in the hall between English and Social Studies. This got you in a bad mood. Also, some kid was in your seat when you went into the room. This got you even more upset. You were telling him to get out of your seat when Mr. Miller came in. He got on your back; and that was too much. You said some things and he said some things and you ended up in the office. It went down hill from there and you're now on suspension. Do I have it right?"

The youngster says, "You have that right. It was Joe's fault."

His parents can then say, "Whose fault it was doesn't make much difference right now. The people at school think it was your fault. It doesn't really matter. Here's the problem. Whoever's fault it was, you're the one with the problem. Let's think about the reasons why you now have a problem and figure out how you can manage and control things differently next time so you don't end up the goat. Of everything that happened, is there one thing that may not have been your best choice? At what point did you have a better choice, had you just thought of it at the time?"

The child's taking responsibility for his behavior can be a slow process but is necessary. The same holds for making better choices and decisions and not trying to blame others for his problems.

Has to Have an Adult Standing Over Him to Get Him to Do His School Work

This can be a sign of several problems. The most likely is that the child has gotten used to only doing his work if an adult is standing over him. Self-discipline, self-direction, responsibility, and the ability to work independently are learned; and the youngster has learned a very bad habit.

Another possible explanation is a need for structure, support, and help. The adult standing over the child is likely to offer suggestions, help keep him on task, and help him organize his work. It seems like the child needs constant supervision but his real need is for help.

Another reason is a little different. Because of hyperactivity, attention deficits, or other learning problems, the child simply cannot settle down and do his work. If these causes are there, he will have other problems his parents will notice, if you help them focus on the possibilities.

Whatever the cause, the child's need for adult supervision is real as is his need to learn to work independently. If his parents watch, they will notice that he can work alone for short periods, maybe only for ten minutes or perhaps only three minutes. The idea is to set an amount of time their child can work alone, without their supervision. They should keep shortening the time until they find an amount of time he can work without their standing over him. It will take a lot of patience, but there is nothing for them to get upset about or frustrated over. If they do, they need to quit for a few minutes. They could say to the youngster, "I need a break. How about you?"

To teach their child to work independently, parents will find that positive rewards work best. Have them determine an amount of time short enough to be sure their child succeeds easily. If there are not other serious problems, ten minutes usually works to start. They then introduce the approach to their child by saying, "If you stay with it for ten minutes right now, you can quit whenever you want after that." The positive reward is getting to quit whenever he wants. He now has control.

They worry that he will not get his work done? He probably will not; but he was not finishing his work anyway. It likely will be some time before he finishes an assignment. Learning to do it himself is the first order of business, though, unless they want to stand over him for the next ten or twenty years.

Feels Teachers and Other Adults at School "Have It In" for Him

First, have parents consider the possibility that their child's perception may be true. At least, he believes it is true. That will be a good place for his parents to start. As you discuss the problem with them, be sure that they do not start by telling him it is not true. He will only see them as unwilling to see his side of things and as just like those teachers who are against him.

Children who are doing well in school seldom have this complaint. Even if they sometimes do, it does not keep them from doing their work. Nonetheless, it may be human nature to feel a little put upon at times, especially when the child has been criticized or did not get something he wanted.

Ask the parents with whom you are talking to suppose that they were reprimanded at work or did not get a job they thought they deserved. Do they think they would say, "The people at work are always reasonable and fair. I had the reprimand coming. I appreciate their honesty with me. I'm a better person for it," or perhaps, "Not getting the job was a fair and reasonable decision. The people for whom I work always do the right thing. This decision is no exception." Children usually handle these kinds of things better than their parents but even kids have their limits.

Instead of arguing or contradicting their child, it would be better for the parents to say, "Okay, the teachers have it in for you. You've told me they aren't doing anything specific; but you can tell. Maybe they just don't like kids or at least some kids. Have I got it right so far?" They can then continue, "They have it in for you; and it keeps you from doing well, from getting the education you tell me you want. Here's the part I don't understand. As angry as you are, it surprises me you're going to let them win, let them stop you from getting an education. It looks like you'd fight back. Do you know how to fight back, how to win?"

They should then listen to see if his ideas would help or if they would make things worse. Likely he will not have an idea. They can then say, "I have some ideas but I think you'd rather be angry and lose. I wonder if you have what it takes to win. What do you think?" If he chooses to quit, it was worth a try. His parents need to understand that his problem goes far beyond feeling picked on.

Disrupts the Classroom or the Activities of Other Children

Parents often see this as a discipline problem and sometimes it is. More commonly, though, it is a sign of learning problems.

Help the child's parents think about his behavior and ask themselves this question. Have they ever seen a child who is doing well in school act like this on any regular basis?

Here is the typical argument many parents make. "If he'd just settle down and behave, he'd do better in school." This is the more accurate point. If he did better in school, he would behave better. Almost always, the learning problem came first and the behavior problem last.

Why does their youngster misbehave? He may have a behavior disorder that needs special treatment. This is so likely, it always needs evaluated by a behavior specialist. Even if he does not have a behavior disorder, it is nearly certain he has a serious learning problem. That, too, needs assessed.

His parents' simply getting on him and pushing him to do better can cause him more problems than he already has. This is a good rule-of-thumb for parents. Until they understand his problems, do not try to fix them and certainly do not permit anyone else who is not a qualified specialist to try to fix them.

Makes No Effort to Cooperate and Get Along

This sign is close to the end of the school and learning line and is an outcome, not the original problem. Typically, it started as a learning problem the child should have gotten help with when he was in the first or second grades. His problem now is a direct result of that long standing learning problem that was not treated.

When the youngster was younger, he likely tried to cooperate and get along. By now, not bothering to try makes sense. How hard do his parents think they would try if they failed almost every day of their lives?

Their helping starts with being honest with their child. They can say, "I think you have a learning problem. I want to try to help. Let me be up-front with you about this. If I were you, I'd probably laugh at anyone who says he wants to help. You've heard that story before. Also, I don't think I'd be much interested in trying if I had your experiences with school and learning. I can't give you any guarantee. I'm just offering to try. Can we talk about it?"

Skips School or Misses School a Lot

Have parents assume that this sign is not because of a medical or physical problem and is not due to a severe emotional or mental illness. If these were the causes, they should be being treated and special arrangements should have been made for the child's education.

Often missing school is the next step beyond not caring. The young person only goes to school when someone makes him go. He might go if he has nothing better to do; and most anything is better from his perspective. This is true, even though he knows that skipping school likely will lead to his dropping out or being expelled.

By now, parents can see how it works. Learning problems have kept their child from being successful at school. He tried but did not succeed.

Over time, his learning problems turned into behavior and attitude problems. They, in turn, led to severe stress and very low self-esteem. These problems led to not caring and perhaps to dropping out or being expelled. At each step along the way, it was easier for his parents and other adults to blame the child and hold him responsible than to understand and help.

If their child has any of the problems discussed in this chapter, advise his parents to talk with his teacher about their concerns. The problems are serious and need attention now. Emphasize with them that if they do not start helping him now, his problems will still be there when school starts again next year and when it starts the year after that. Their child will not simply outgrow the problems. Perhaps they tell you that they do not have time to talk to their child's teacher. If so, have no hesitation to say, "That's a real shame. Your child will have the rest of his life to deal with the consequences of your being too busy to help him today."

CHAPTER 5

SERIOUS BEHAVIOR PROBLEMS

Overview

Suppose a child is 16 and has not learned to cooperate and get along. He does what he wants, when he wants, where he wants, how he wants, with whom he wants to do it. Have the parents with whom you are talking use the following illustration as a case in point as you focus their attention on how likely Randy's parents would be today to get him to cooperate and behave more appropriately.

> No one can tell how Randy is going to be from one minute to the next. Sometimes he is almost nice; but usually he is in a bad mood and hard to get along with. Anything can set him off.
>
> This morning before school is a perfect example. Sue and Bret are coming in from the bus talking and minding their own business. For no reason, Randy yells, "Hey stupid!" to Bret and then says something to Sue only she and Randy hear. Whatever it is, it embarrasses Sue and Bret says something back to Randy. That is all Randy needs.
>
> It looks like Bret would know to just keep his mouth shut. Everyone knows how Randy is. We don't want to repeat what Randy says; but he can be heard screaming all over the building.
>
> When Mr. Richards arrives, Sue is crying. Bret is on the floor holding his head; and Randy is standing around acting like the whole thing is Bret's fault.

Now have the parents imagine that Randy is their child. They need to try to get him to cooperate whether they think they will succeed or not. What approach will they use?

Some parents take the *tough guy* approach. They are going to knock some sense into that boy. Here is how one father fared with the tough guy approach.

> Butch shoves clean clothes into his duffel bag and tries to sneak out the hall door where he can leave by the outside cellar stairs without going through the kitchen. His father is fed up with him and has grounded him. This time, the crisis has been precipitated by an incident between Butch and his mother; and Leroy (Butch's father) has, at his wife's urging, stepped in to handle Butch.

There is no way Butch is going to put up with that from either of them. He'll get out of there however he has to do it.

He almost makes it; but just as he starts to open the hall door to go down to the cellar, Leroy yells, "Get your hand off that door. You're not going out of this house. Put down that bag and get your ass back into your room."

Butch drops the bag, opens the cellar door, and starts down. Before he is on the first step, Leroy jerks him back and is between him and his escape. "Who do you think you are? If you think you can just waltz out of here, you've got another thing coming to you; and I'm just the man who can give it to you."

Butch has grown past six feet tall and is looking down at his father now. Leroy stretches up to scream louder in Butch's face. Butch reaches for Leroy, for his throat. There is a hint of panic as Leroy says, "You keep your hands off me. You just try it and I'll kick your ass all the way up between your ears. Any day you think you can handle the old man, you just try it."

Butch's rage is blind. The violence that has been building within him for years is no longer to be suppressed. He forces his hands under Leroy's arms, lifts him off the floor, and slams him against the door jam. As Leroy falls, he swings at Butch who catches the blow with his arm. With blind fury, Butch's fist crashes into Leroy's face once, twice, three times; and Leroy slumps and staggers back. Butch sees what is happening but does not reach to help as Leroy tumbles down the cellar stairs.

Can the parents with whom you are talking agree that Leroy's approach did not work out at all well for either him or Butch? Here is what parents often miss. The problem is not the outcome. It would not have been any better if Leroy had knocked Butch down the cellar stairs. The problem was Leroy's tough guy approach.

When Butch was younger and would get into it with his mother, Leroy simply pulled him up by the scruff of the neck and threw him into his room. When Butch was a little boy, his mother was strong enough and big enough to get the job done by herself. Back then, Leroy usually just stood by and watched.

The tough guy[20] approach is never appropriate. Getting children to cooperate and get along is not a matter of who has the most power or who is bigger and stronger, although that approach may appear to work for a while. Eventually, the children get older, stronger, smarter, and able to take care of themselves. If not, they frequently become the victims of someone else who can abuse and bully them. Either way, the tough guy approach leads to the kids' missing the opportunity to learn how to successfully resolve conflict, how to behave reasonably and appropriately.

---

[20]This should not be confused with "tough love" which is an approach that emphasizes setting strict limits but does not involve physical aggression or violence.

Signs of Serious Behavior Problems

As you think with parents about these signs of serious behavior problems, do not overlook the good news. Most kids do not have serious behavior problems. They have better days and worse days; but on the whole, they are growing and learning fine. Importantly, they are learning to cooperate and get along without the use of tough guy approaches.

Some children do have serious behavior problems; and for the most part, these kids also have other serious difficulties. The most common additional difficulty is a serious learning problem. In fact, it is unusual to see a serious behavior problem in a child who does not have learning difficulties. If parents answer "Yes" to any of the following questions, their child has or is developing serious behavior problems.[21] He likely also has other problems needing careful professional attention. It is unlikely that his parents can help him with his behavior problems without working on the other difficulties too. This work always needs to include the participation of a behavior specialist.

Caution parents to be careful when selecting such a specialist. Not every professional who works successfully with children and adolescents has the experience and expertise to effectively help with seriously behavior disordered children.

Does Their Child:

- Frequently pout and become very difficult to live with?
- Become nasty and hateful?
- Get extremely angry when things do not go his way?
- Often scream and yell at people?
- Break or damage things?
- Intentionally hit or hurt people (or animals)?
- Start or get into fights?
- Bully and pick on others?
- Treat people cruelly?
- Refuse to follow parental rules or behave like his parents expect?
- Refuse to accept the authority of parents, teachers, or other adults in charge?

---

[21]It often helps to think of a child's behavior problems as an unfortunate side-affect of his maladaptive, unfruitful search for a way to relate to or get along with others, to find his role or position, to fit in and belong specifically with peers and generally within his world. Helping him fundamentally involves helping him appropriately achieve these outcomes.

- Often behave in socially inappropriate ways?
- Use or have other involvements with illegal drugs, including alcohol? (Keep in mind that alcohol is an illegal drug where kids are concerned.)
- Have friends who often get into trouble?
- Have a reputation for not being someone others can depend on or trust?
- Seem not to care if he upsets or hurts people?
- Repeatedly get into trouble with the police or courts?

Pouts and Becomes Very Difficult to Live With

All children have some way of handling it when they don't get their way. They have their own ways of reacting when things do not work out as they want. They have ways of dealing with a world they think is sometimes unfair.

Two of their choices are temper tantrums and pouting. Most children use one or the other of these once in a while; and if parents watch their child, they likely will see that he uses one more than the other.

Just to be fair, have the parents answer this question. "When you get angry or frustrated, are you more likely to pout or have a little temper tantrum?" If they do not know or think that they do neither, have them ask someone at their home what they think. They will quickly tell them whether they are a pouter or temper tantrum thrower.

Now, have the parents take a minute to think about a child who neither pouts nor has temper tantrums. This can be much worse than either pouting or temper tantrums because it often means the child is just accepting whatever happens. Even worse, he has gotten to where he no longer has any feelings about what happens to him. He does not care or thinks what he feels does not matter. Help his parents understand that this would be a very unhealthy place for their child to be both emotionally and interpersonally.

What is their child doing when he pouts? He is angry, frustrated, or upset about something; but his predominate feeling is anger. He does not talk about it or try to work out his problem. Instead, he pouts and makes it rough for his parents and other people who are around him.

Encourage his parents to think about what upset him. Maybe what happened was unfair and he really was treated badly. Either way, his pouting about it is a problem.

Based on their thinking about what might have set off their child's pouting behavior, they can say, "I've thought about what happened. We can talk about it if you want to. Here's my problem right now. You have a right to feel how you feel but pouting about it isn't your best choice. I think it'd be better if you either got up-and-over it or at least talked about it. It's your choice. This is what I'm going to do. I'm going to do nothing unless you choose to talk with me about it. You can pout or talk. It's your choice. If you choose to pout, please do it in your room." Now they need to leave it alone. His only choice is to behave more appropriately or be by himself.

Becomes Nasty and Hateful

Children get in a bad mood once in a while. Even so, it is not acceptable to take it out on everyone around. Instead, it is a good opportunity for kids to get better at managing their thoughts, feelings, and relationships. An approach that is usually fairly difficult but helpful for parents is to leave their child's bad mood alone at first. They can offer to talk with him about his bad feelings but should not make any effort to cheer him up. He will be happier when he is happier.

Parents' objective should be to deal only with their child's hatefulness. It usually comes off as cutting remarks, putting people down, and being angry. Teach them to focus their efforts and energy on helping him better manage these strong feelings.

As they interact with their child, difficult as it will be, they need to resist any urge to react to his hatefulness by being hateful and angry with him. Support them in their efforts to stay calm and not take the youngster's hatefulness personally. It probably has little to do with them.

Parents should talk with their child about what is really going on. They can say, "Here's the real problem. When you say and do things that are so hateful, it really hurts. Right now, you feel like you are the one who has been hurt. I know that and so do you. Hurting me and other people isn't your best choice, though. I'm going to try very hard not to hurt you even if you feel you need to hurt me. Maybe one of these days, you will not need to take your hurt out on others. Until then, please think about it. Here's an idea. If you can tell me about what's bothering you, maybe we can figure out something to help."

If their child will not talk and persists in being hateful, they might want to try isolating the youngster. They can have him go to his room or another room of the house until he has thought about his behavior and is able to interact less hatefully. If he returns in the same mood, they can send him back to his room and then talk with him about his behavior before he is permitted to be with others in the home. If this approach is used, the need to remain calm and non-confrontational is still present. The temptation for most parents is to get angry and to try to force their child to behave better. This normally will not work and only tends to make matters worse. They first need to set a good example for him and assertively tell him that his behavior is not acceptable to them.

They are teaching their child better ways to handle his angry feelings. Once they have control of their personal reactions and emotions, they can begin letting him know when they notice that he is doing better. Over time, his moods, attitudes, and behavior will change in the direction of the behavior they are modeling for him.

Gets Extremely Angry When Things Do Not Go His Way

This is the temper tantrum side of anger and frustration. Children get frustrated and upset when things do not go their way; and as with most problems, it is a matter of how much. The problem is not so much the child's reaction itself as it is how angry he gets and how he expresses his anger.

Parents need to help their child feel okay about being angry or frustrated; but at the same time, he needs to manage his anger better. His parents need to teach him more appropriate ways to handle his anger and frustration without their getting angry, without their threatening him. The key is for them to model more appropriate behavior for him.

With preschool children, it is true that ignoring temper tantrums often works. They then come up with more appropriate ways to let their parents know how they feel. If tantrums still are their usual way of managing their anger and frustration by six to seven-years-old, though, they certainly have developed an effective way to let their parents know when they are mad; and they have learned the wrong behavior. Ignoring them is no longer their parents' best choice, were ignoring them even possible any more.

Whenever they can, parents should avoid dealing with the temper tantrum while it is happening. Doing anything then only makes matters worse. Tantrums take a lot of energy and can only last about so long; and their child cannot keep it up forever. They should wait calmly until his anger lessens, and it will. They can then say, "You've used a tantrum to say something to me. I do (or don't) understand what you were trying to say. Here's my point. I don't do anything about things when told about them in such an angry way. Let's try again. If you want to say something to me and want me to do something about it, tell me more calmly. Help me understand what has you so upset. What do you want to tell me and what do you want me to do about it?"

It is important to emphasize with parents that they should not try to talk or reason with their child while he is having the tantrum. They should wait until he calms. If necessary, they should leave the room or have him leave the room until he settles. Only after he is calmer should they ask about what is so upsetting for him.

Screams and Yells at People

Over a week or so, have parents make a note every time anyone in their home screams or yells at someone. It will be easier for them to help their child if they see that he is not the only one who is behaving inappropriately. If they have a quiet family, then have them count the times anyone raises his voice or talks harshly to someone. This is their brand of screaming and yelling.

The activity will help them see that the specific child's behavior is inappropriate only by degrees. He yells and screams too loudly, too much, too long, and at the wrong times. He over does it. That is what his problem actually is.

His parents need to start their helping process by being sure no one yells and screams at him when he yells at someone. Each person in their family needs to take responsibility for how he handles the child's behavior. At a family meeting, his parents can set the rules. They can say, for example, "Kevin has a problem with screaming and yelling. We all are going to help him learn better ways to say what he has to say. Let's agree to do this. Any time Kevin yells at one of us, he or she will wait patiently until the yelling stops. Say this to him. 'If you've finished yelling, I'd like to hear what you want to say to me. Will you tell me in a more appropriate way?' " The parents just need to be sure they are ready to be good campers when their four-year-old reminds them about the family rules by saying to one of them, "No yelling. I only listen when you talk right."

Breaks and Damages Things

This sign depends on whether breaking and damaging things is accidental, unintentional, or on purpose. These are three different problems. If the youngster often breaks things by accident, it is probably a physical problem. It may involve coordination, vision, or another medical problem that needs to be evaluated by a physician.

Unintentionally breaking things is a little harder to understand. It may be because of not knowing how to use toys and equipment. Encourage parents to think about why it happens and see if teaching their child how to use things correctly might work better than forbidding him to use whatever he broke.

Unintentionally breaking or intentionally breaking things are sometimes degrees of the same behavior. The child feels upset, angry, or wants to get even. He is careless and too rough with others' things and may intentionally break them. He may behave the same way with his things, taking out his anger and frustration on objects. Whatever the focus of his aggression, the behavior is a kind of temper tantrum.

Although it is extraordinarily difficult, it is usually better for parents of a child exhibiting this behavior to calmly watch while he breaks whatever it is, unless the child or someone else might be hurt. Most of the time, they cannot stop him anyway. He can always break it when they are not there to do anything about it.

There are several things parents can do. If their child can, he should pay for what he broke. If his parents use this approach, they need to avoid taking away all his money for very long. It is better for them to set up payments their child can afford.

Further, it usually helps not to replace what he broke if it belonged to him; but caution his parents to be careful. They do not want him to end up with nothing but junk. He needs to see his things as valuable before not breaking them will matter to him.

Each time he breaks something, his parents should talk with him about how he felt. Their goal is to get their child to talk about how he felt angry, jealous, or frustrated. They can say, "Your breaking things is a problem. At least you reached your goal. If you broke them to cause someone a problem, you got the job done. That lets me know you can communicate. Here's what I want to talk about. There are better ways to let people know how you feel. For example, yelling or pounding your pillow would be better. They aren't long-term solutions but are in the right direction. Can we talk about some choices you have that are better than breaking things?" Help the child's parents understand that their having this discussion with him as often as necessary is important. They need to have it each time the problem occurs. That will be easier if you share this technique with them. Have them have this discussion when neither they nor their child is upset or angry. This may mean that they will need to wait a while to give both them and their child a chance to settle.

Intentionally Hits and Hurts People (or Animals)

Children who have been abused or who have experienced domestic violence learned this behavior from adults who took it to the extreme. Parents who think that it is acceptable to spank and slap their children are modeling the same behavior in a milder form. They teach their kids, by example, that hitting and hurting are acceptable if one does not hit too hard or hurt too much. It is the same unacceptable lesson for the child, though. Be sure that parents with whom you are talking are not teaching this behavior to their child through hitting and hurting him.

When parents observe the sign in their child, encourage them to stop the child from hitting and hurting without themselves becoming aggressive with him. Their intervention should follow this progression:

- First, ask him to stop.
- Next, insist he stops.
- If necessary, restrain him from the behavior if this can be comfortably done without a struggle or physical confrontation.
- Whenever possible, parents should avoid trying to physically stop their child's unacceptable behavior while it is happening.

As with other behavior problems, the child's parents setting a good example for him is essential; and they need to insist that everyone in their family does the same. This will likely require their teaching others to back off when he gets upset and angry. No, this does not mean he gets his way. It only means that everyone agrees not to push when he cannot control himself. The youngster will calm down after a while. In the interim, everyone should try to stay out of his angry space.

As a parallel process, the child's parents should try giving him small rewards for good days; days when he does not hit or hurt. A treat, special privilege, or something he wants all help. The key for his parents is to use negative reactions very sparingly. The payoff for their child needs to be for appropriate behavior, for not hitting and hurting.

As you talk with his parents about the intervention process, take extra care to be sure they do not omit this additional step. They should always make a point to talk to their child after he has behavior difficulty. The approach is to sit quietly with him while he calms down. They can then talk about his angry feelings and how he managed them. He needs to learn to pick up on the clues that he is about to lose control.

Teach them to say, "Once you get angry, stopping is very hard. You can learn to stop; but it's tough. It's easier to stop if you catch it before you lose control. If we can figure out when you first started to get upset, that's the place to control it, the best time to manage your anger better and come up with another way to express it. When did it first start getting to you?"

Their goal is for their child to spot situations and people that set him off. The best time for him to get control and to learn emotional management is while he still has control. As he learns to anticipate[22] situations, his control will get better.

Simply to emphasize a point previously made, if the initial efforts of parents are not successful (or exceed their capacity) and if their child's behavior is not improving, getting specialized help is essential. You can help them identify a qualified family therapist who will assist them in working through the interpersonal and behavior problems you and they have identified.

Starts and Gets Into Fights

This is a two-sided problem. Children may bully and pick on other kids and start fights; or they may come out fighting any time they get frustrated, angry, or afraid. Conversely, some children may do things that aggravate others to the point of fighting. Either way, it is a serious problem.

Several things need some thought. Where did the child learn the behavior? Whether he is the aggressor or the victim, he learned the role somewhere. It is not true children often fight. By ten or so, most youngsters never get into physical fights. Those who do usually have a behavior problem. They think that fighting is a good way to settle things. They may have learned this from their families or perhaps from living in their neighborhoods or attending their schools. Some places are very rough; and fighting is the normal way to handle conflict. Finally, it may just be one step beyond screaming and yelling, hitting and hurting. If these

[22]Children learn to anticipate situations at an empirical or "thinking" level as well as at an emotional or visceral level. They learn to "feel" it coming. Learning at this level is subjective and requires coaching and experiential approaches. This is sometimes called intuitive learning and must come from adults who can meaningfully discuss intuitive processes.

problems go unchecked, fighting and more serious violence are nearly certain, especially as the children get physically bigger and stronger.

If parents are at their wits end and their child still fights, encourage them to say, "Your fighting is a serious problem. We've tried several things over many weeks. (They should then list the things they have tried.) You're still fighting. Here's the problem. I want to help you but wonder if I can. However you feel about it, I want you to know where I stand. If you and I can't work this out, it still has to be worked out. The fighting has to stop. We'll start with counseling. If that doesn't help, we'll take the next step. I don't know for sure right now what that is. I sincerely hope we don't have to find out; but I want you to know that I will do whatever it takes to help you."

What if the youngster says, "I don't care what you do?" His parents can say, "That's a shame. I wish you cared. I care and will do what has to be done to help you over this problem. Nothing is happening today so we'll have some chances to talk about this more."

Bullies and Picks on Others

This is worse than just fighting. Usually it is caused by the child's insecurity and low self-esteem. He needs to bully and act powerful to hide the fear and self-doubt that underlie the behavior. Less common is a child who just likes to hurt people and control them. When this is what is going on, the young person is extremely disturbed.[23]

Parents need to watch their child, his behavior, and his reactions. Focus their attention on these questions;

- Does he want to be one up and more powerful than other children?
- Does he get pleasure from seeing other children suffer?

These questions are not the same and it does make a difference. If the young person's need is to be one-up and in control, his parents can normally help. Their child wants other kids to respect him and like him but has picked a way that does not work. They are afraid of him but neither respect him nor like him much. His parents can say, for example, "Bullying and picking on Susie isn't a good way to get the respect you want. It just makes her afraid of you and causes others not to like you. It

[23]When a child seems to enjoy hurting and controlling other children, consider the possibility that he is being mistreated in the same way at home. When away from home, he assumes the "power" role with others. If this is happening, he is being abused at home and is behaving as he was taught. You will need to separately address this issue.

doesn't get you what you want. Even those who act like they think you are a big deal aren't being honest with you. They're using you to feel important. Some of them are afraid and don't want you to treat them the way you treat Susie. You'll have to decide whether you want to be a bully or have people like you."

The child may say that he does not care whether anyone likes him. If so, his parents can go on to say, "It's your choice. I'm just saying being a bully is not your best choice if you want people to be friends with you. You have choices. If you're interested, I'll think with you about some of those choices." Be sure the child's parents do not miss the opportunity to teach but carefully resist the temptation to preach.

Treats People Cruelly

This is the end of the anger road. The behavior has become an end in itself. The child's hurting someone because he was angry with them was a serious problem; but hurting them just to see them suffer is very disturbed behavior.

Although a little teasing and tormenting usually are only good fun, too much is a serious problem. It works like this. When children are about five or six, they begin to see things as others see them. It is as if they momentarily become the other person and feel what they feel. This is called empathy. By grade school, they do this fairly automatically most of the time. One value of empathy is knowing when other people are hurting physically or emotionally. If they are, the child feels badly and wants to help. This is how he tells when enough teasing and tormenting are enough. When it stops being fun and starts hurting, enough is enough. Knowing just when to stop is a problem; but most children know about where the line is and respect it.

Children who are intentionally cruel and get pleasure from the behavior are across the line. They want to see the other person suffer. Empathy or the pain of the other person does not stop the behavior. Usually, children showing this sign have themselves been victims of abusive behavior and have well-learned what they were taught.

An important point for parents to take to heart is to be sure that no one in their home torments their child physically or emotionally. Further, they should keep teasing to a minimum and are responsible to assure that no one tries to retaliate against their child when he does something for which others may want retribution. Neither parents nor anyone else in the family should try to teach him a lesson by hurting him. He needs gentleness, firm guidance, and a predictable family. The parents' primary approach needs to be talking with him about his behavior, the feelings and pain of others, and about his angry emotions.

A related sign involves sexually aggressive behavior. This is usually perpetrated by boys on girls but may involve kids of either sex with kids of either sex. Typically, the behavior involves an older or bigger youngster forcing sexual involvement with a younger or smaller child. The key is the element of coercion and the inability of the victim to stop or prevent the behavior. If parents discuss this type of behavior with you, it is critically important that you take it very seriously. It is not a "kids will be kids" kind of thing and often indicates a serious behavior disorder requiring immediate, specialized attention.[24] At a minimum, the parents need to discuss the behavior with a specialist in the area of children's sexually disordered behavior, keeping in mind that most "therapists" are not experts in this area. Similarly, the victim of sexually aggressive behavior needs specialized help too. Most therapists who work successfully with children have expertise with victims.

Refuses to Follow the Rules or Behave Like Parents or Other Adults Expect

It is unusual to see a child who lives in a home where there are reasonable rules and who is following those rules but having severe behavior problems at school or in the community. Putting this another way, children who cooperate with and get along with their parents seldom get into repeated trouble away from home. Youngsters first learn to cooperate and get along at home; and if they do not, they likely will have serious problems away from home.

The first question to ask parents whose child exhibits this sign is whether they have rules and expectations for the child. Most parents would be surprised to know how often youngsters are left to fend for themselves. Basically they are allowed to do whatever they want, whenever they want, with whomever they want so long as they do not bother anyone at home. They have few rules and little supervision. That combination is a nearly certain way to end up with a child with serious behavior problems. Children who have not been taught to behave do not behave very well.

---

[24]Be sensitive to the possibility that sexually aggressive behavior may be a product of the child's being sexually abused, either directly or by exposure to the sexually aggressive behavior of others. If this type of suspicion is present for you, you need to deal with it as a separate issue, including reporting your suspicions to child protective personnel.

Next, children develop serious behavior problems in homes where the rules are on-again, off-again. Sometimes they can do as they please and other times nothing they do is right. Sometimes their parents ignore their behavior and sometimes the reactions the kids get are out of proportion to anything the child did or did not do. This pattern is often seen in homes where there is violence, alcohol and drug abuse, adults moving in and out, or illegal activity. It also is seen in homes where the adults have serious behavior problems. There, the children learn to behave just like one or both of their parents.

Alternatively, youngsters with this type of maladjustment sometimes grow up in homes where the rules and expectations are simply unreasonable. They cannot follow the rules and cannot get along. Also, the same difficulty comes up if the child has other problems that keep him from being able to do what is expected. For example, learning or serious emotional problems can keep a child from doing what people expect. In this case, the expectations are actually unreasonable for the specific child.

If the child is not following his parents' rules, then, these questions need answered.

- Do the child's parents have rules and expectations he understands and can follow?
- Do the rules stay the same, without changing unpredictably?
- Does the child get positive feedback when he follows his parents' rules?
- Does not following his parents' rules consistently lead to negative feedback the child can understand and handle?

His parents need to understand that discipline needs to be there; but it needs to be consistent, in proportion to what happened, and not just another version of the tough guy approach. Help them see that it is better to ask their child what should happen when he does not follow one of their family's rules. Youngsters often have suggestions that are both reasonable and appropriate. Family discussions about rules also can serve as an important part of the child's learning to cooperate and get along.

Refuses to Accept the Authority of Parents, Teachers, or Others in Charge

Helping parents understand this sign when they see it in their child can be hard because there is a lot of difference between authority and power. Children learn to respect authority, people in authority, and learn to accept authority. This becomes a value. Power is different. It gets its importance from who is bigger and stronger. Power is something to fear; and people with power are to be feared.

How a child sees his parents, teachers, and other adults is important. Does he see them as someone in authority or as someone with power? The youngster may say, "You can't make me do it." That is what he literally means. "You can't or won't use power to make me do it." He likely is right.

Have the child's parents say, "You're right. Even if I could make you do it, I won't. I won't treat you that way. I'll help you learn it's better for you to do what I ask than to refuse; but you can still refuse. Please do what I ask so we don't have to figure out what other choices we have. Just understand that there are other choices."

Often Behaves in Socially Inappropriate Ways

Help parents to think about whether their child really knows the socially appropriate ways to behave. Their simply telling him is not, by itself, enough. He needs to try, behave inappropriately, try again, and perhaps behave inappropriately again. Like other children, he also will sometimes act badly even though he knows better. Help his parents understand that their goal should be successive approximations. This means that their child comes closer to what they expect as time goes on. No child always behaves well. His parents' goal should only be for him to act more appropriately more of the time, as time goes on.

They need additionally to be sure that they and others at home are setting good examples of appropriate behavior. A specific child likely will not behave any better than others in his family.

Uses Illegal Drugs

This is a very complicated problem. A useful place to start as you advise parents is to encourage them to think about it in terms of values: right and wrong, good and bad. If the value of following the law, avoiding dangerous things, and doing what is right is stronger, the youngster likely says, "No." If not, the ubiquitous peer pressure to use illegal drugs likely wins.

Parents whose child is using "drugs" need to resist the temptation to react to the problem by getting angry and lecturing him. Most importantly, they should not threaten him. Teach them to say instead, "It'll be a great day when you understand that you're important enough and valuable enough to treat yourself better. It'll be a better day when you don't run the risk of hurting yourself with alcohol and drugs. You deserve better."

Further, be sure parents resist doing anything to protect their child from the consequences that his drug use causes. If he has problems with the police, they are his problems. If he gets into trouble at school, it is his trouble. Protecting him from the natural and logical consequences of his behavior only supports the behavior. Of course, the youngster needs specialized drug treatment services provided by qualified child-experts. Nonetheless, his accepting responsibility for his behavior and actions includes experiencing the full consequences of that behavior.

An additional point is important. Too often, parents find out about or strongly suspect their child's drug or alcohol use and either say nothing to him or have "a little talk" and do nothing else. Drug and alcohol problems are too serious to simply be left to chance. Encourage them to talk with their child anytime they are concerned. If their suspicions persist or recur, encourage them to, at a minimum, discuss their observations and concerns with a specialist who works primarily with young people who have substance abuse problems.

Has Friends Who Often Get into Trouble

This is hard for parents to prevent and harder for them to deal with. When children pick their friends, they choose people who they think are like them or are like they want to be. What if their child sees himself as a loser, as not belonging in the in-group? He will then choose his friends from the out-group, since his need to belong "drives" him toward whomever will accept him. These are the youngsters who are having more than their share of problems and are more than likely getting into trouble. Their child may just hang around with anyone who will accept him or at least not reject him. The out-group is not choosy. They will let anyone hang around who goes along and does not act like he thinks he is better than they are. They are an easy home-base for children with low self-esteem and behavior problems.

The youngster's parents telling him that he cannot hang around with those kids does little good. They likely cannot stop him; and if they do, he may then have no friends. The children his parents like and of whom they approve will not let him into their group. This is a fact of life in the real world of children. He is only accepted by other youngsters with serious problems just when his need to belong is strongest.

Their child is in a nearly impossible bind. He wants friends, has to have friends; but his friends have more problems than he does. What can his parents or the youngster do? Along with getting professional help, they and he can talk honestly about the bind.

Suggest that the youngster's parents try this approach. "Here is the problem. You're having some serious behavior problems. I know that and so do you. Now, your friends also have serious problems. You and I know that's true whether they know it or not. For you, the problem is getting into trouble when you're around them. That's when you have most of your problems. Can we agree that you get into trouble mostly when you are with your friends? If so, we have a place to start. I don't have any answers but think this is where to start looking for some. What ideas do you have?"

Support the child's parents in their coming to understand that there are no magic solutions or quick fixes. They and he need to keep talking about it. Arguing about any of it is not going to help. If it could, the problem would be gone for it is nearly certain that the child and his parents have done enough arguing to fix a thousand problems if arguing were the answer.

A related circumstance is a child's being suspected of or becoming involved with a *gang*.[25] This is a growing problem in all communities. It will enhance your ability to talk knowledgeably with parents if you take a proactive approach to learning as much as you can about gangs and gang-related behavior in your area. The police are usually your best resource. They can tell you about the extent of local gang activity, signs parents should watch for that indicate that their child may be associated with a particular gang, and specialized resources for children who exhibit signs of possible gang involvement. Be sure that parents do not consult with anyone who is not a locally recognized expert in gang-related behavior. It is a specialized area of practice in which most therapists are not experts. It also is useful to know that most children who are involved with a gang will not deny their involvement, if asked. They may but normally do not. Their parents should ask, if they suspect involvement; but they also need to pursue their concerns, if their suspicions persist.

---

[25]Gangs answer the need of some children for affiliation and belonging, including somewhere to belong and a valued identity in a very concrete sense.

Has a Reputation for Not Being Someone Others Can Depend on or Trust

This sign gets to the nub of the child's value problems. When he does not have solid values, it is much harder for his parents and others who interact with him to know how he is going to act and what he is going to do. This makes it very tough for his parents to have a good relationship with him and tougher to live with him.

It is a vicious circle. The child's potentials and life experiences led to insufficient development within his moral dimension. This may be because no one adequately taught him or because his learning problems or other life-experiences made it unusually difficult for him to learn value-related principles and concepts. Learning problems are not limited to books and school. They can negatively affect learning within each dimension of the child's development and can cause problems in most any situation or circumstance.

The youngster's developmental problems led to his being undependable and not trustworthy. Most everyone sees him this way and wants nothing to do with him. There is no payoff for him to work to keep relationships he does not have with people who do not like him anyway.

The child will not work to get better relationships since he does not have any experience telling him that he can form satisfying relationships or that having them is worth the effort. Consequently, he does not change; and people continue rejecting him. It gets worse as time goes on and as he gets older. Around and around the vicious circle goes for him.

Focus your advice for his parents on their relying on logical and natural consequences. For example, instead of trying to correct his unacceptable behavior at school or in the community, the child's parents should let "the system" respond to his behavior. His parents' task is to be sure that they are not minimizing the seriousness of the problem or interfering with others who are doing what is called for within the context of their responsibilities. Their child needs to experience the full consequences of his unacceptable behavior.

This approach will work with a couple exceptions. First, he will usually think that the consequences occurred because of bad luck and not because of his behavior. Taking responsibility is not his thing, so to speak. Second, parents cannot let everyone reject their child. If they do, he may be permanently lost into the empty world of the socially and emotionally outcast. They need to hang in there with him, even though they neither like nor approve of his behavior.

As you encourage the youngster's parents to find within themselves all the patience, faith, and hope they can, it will help them to know this. Just maybe, he may come to value their relationship more than his unacceptable behavior. It is worth a try. Hanging in there may not be quite the logical thing; but if they were all that logical, they likely would not be parents in the first place. For them, loving and caring for their child are at least as important as is logic.

When you refer the child's parents to a specialist, and you will, two points need attention. First, serious behavior problems are usually best treated through a combination of evaluating the learning difficulties that are typically present, and group counseling. Children with serious behavior problems normally do better in group treatment than in individual therapy. Second, family therapy or at least the serious involvement of the child's parents is necessary. The youngster's treatment will not be more than minimally successful without the participation of his parents.

Does Not Care if He Upsets or Hurts People

What would a child be like without values? He would not care about anyone or anything but himself and might not even care much about himself and about what he becomes. The extreme version of this is not caring if he hurts people.

The youngster's parents may have already gotten this advice: "Don't let him know he hurt you. Don't let him get under your skin. If he does, act like he didn't." The normally well-meaning advice is not to let him know he won.

Here is the point you should have his parents make with their child. He hurt them and upset them a lot. They do not honestly let him know this truth by getting angry with him, hurting him, or by withdrawing from him. He needs his parents to frankly let him know how it feels to them in adult terms.

Teach them to say, "What you said (or did) upset me. It hurts way down inside. It's an awful feeling. It feels like I was just pushed off a cliff and am falling. I'm afraid. It may be the worst feeling I've ever had. I'm really suffering."

He likely will say that he does not care. Coach them to then say, "That makes me feel even worse. Your not caring is worse for me than what happened. You don't need to say or do anything about it. I just want you to know how much I am hurting."

Will they ever get through to him? It is certain that by not trying, they will never get through to him. He needs their caring and honesty, straight-up and to the point.

Gets into Trouble With the Police or Courts

Any child might get into trouble once with the police or have to go to court. It might not be a sign of serious trouble. The youngster learns and does not find himself back in the same fix. This sign only applies to children who get into trouble over and over again.

If their child is exhibiting this type of repetitively delinquent behavior, his parents can hope that the court will do what it needs to do. He will get some of those logical and natural consequences. At least, this is what typically will happen unless his parents try to talk the court out of taking appropriate action. Your advice to them needs to serve to prevent them from trying to intercede or lessen the judgement of the court. It is time for the young person to "face the music." Beyond your attempting to prevent his parents from interfering with the court process, they need to focus their care and attention on helping improve his self-esteem. They do this by working with him on his social skills and on the serious learning problems he likely has.

The child, his parents, and the specialists you have helped them identify, should work on the causes of his behavior and adjustment problems. The courts and community will help him understand the logical and natural consequences of his unacceptable behavior.[26]

[26]Although youngsters who are severely behaviorally maladjusted also have self-esteem difficulties, they often appear to have very high self-esteem. They believe that their attitudes and behavior are fine and feel a sense of pride in their deviance. This pattern represents a level of behavioral intransigence that is extraordinarily impermeable to therapeutic interventions.

CHAPTER 6

INTERPERSONAL MALADJUSTMENT

Overview

To shift the parents' focus away from their child's specific behavior and toward his interpersonal adjustment, have them consider the following illustration.

> Joe's mother and father are sitting at the dinner table talking after Joe and his brother, Terry, have eaten and left the kitchen. "I'm worried about Joe," his mother says as Mr. Butler pours his wife another cup of coffee. He sits, waiting until she continues, "It's hard to put my finger on it. He just seems to have lost interest in his friends and the things he had seemed to enjoy. I guess I don't know if he has any friends anymore. He talks on the phone sometimes but I don't think he does much with anyone. He just stays in his room and does things he can do by himself. He seemed to be getting along fine. At least, I hadn't noticed anything until lately. I don't know what happened. I really am concerned."
>
> Mr. Butler thinks about what his wife said and then says, "I know what you mean. It may be even more of a problem than you're saying. I know Terry asked him to shoot some baskets and he said he was too busy. All he did was watch television. I don't know if you have noticed it or not but the last few times someone has called him, he's made some excuse not to talk with them. Have you said anything to him about what you're feeling?"
>
> Mrs. Butler does not know what to say. She finally says, "I've tried to talk to him. He says everything's fine and I'm making too much of a deal out of it. He brushes it off and won't talk about what he's thinking. He just shuts me out. He acts like he doesn't have a care in the world. I don't know. I'm worried."

Joe's case is an example of how interpersonal problems can catch parents by surprise. Had their child never developed good social skills or if he had always had trouble getting along with people, they would know there is a problem and would likely know why. It would still be something needing their caring attention but would not be so surprising.

The surprise comes when parents find themselves in the situation in which Joe's parents found themselves. Things are fine; and then one day they find themselves wondering what is going on. Things with their child do not seem quite right. It is hard to put their finger on exactly what is wrong; but they are concerned.

Parents should trust their intuitions. Something has changed and they and their child need to think about it, talk about it, understand the change. Being familiar with the common signs of interpersonal maladjustment will help as you facilitate parents' focusing on their child's difficulties and understand what is happening.

Signs of Interpersonal Maladjustment

As you help parents think about these signs of interpersonal maladjustment, keep in mind that most youngsters do not have these difficulties on any continuing basis. They have better days and worse days; but on the whole, they are developing satisfactorily and getting along fine interpersonally.

Some kids do have problems with people and relationships, though. For the most part, these youngsters also are having other difficulties. The most common additional difficulty is a serious change in the youngster's self-esteem. In fact, it is unusual to see serious, interpersonal maladjustment in a child who does not have self-esteem difficulties.

This is the point to make with the youngster's parents. Something is going on in their child's world that is causing him to have trouble getting along with people. If he has not always had trouble, something is going on now. What has changed? What happened at school or somewhere else to cause problems with his friends? What is not working as well for him as it had been? The cause is there if you can help his parents be patient enough and persistent enough to find it. The likelihood is that the youngster already knows exactly what changed. The question is whether his parents can help him feel safe enough to share it with them.

If parents answer "yes" to any of the following questions, their child is or is becoming interpersonally maladjusted. They need to proceed gently but persistently.

The signs that follow are divided into three groups. The first group deals with problems getting along with other children. The second focuses on difficulties related to low self-esteem; and the third considers signs of withdrawal and isolation. As you talk with parents, it is important to consider all three areas in order to fully explore the types and range of interpersonal maladjustment children may exhibit.

Does Their Child:

- Try to keep his friends all to himself?
- Often get his feelings hurt?
- Often become the brunt of teasing and put-downs?
- Get up-tight and nervous when someone is angry or upset?
- Refuse to stick up for himself?
- Try to please everyone and keep everyone happy?
- Feel like most people do not like him?
- Get rejected or ignored by most people his age?

* * * * * *

- Worry and fret about not doing things well enough and about failing?
- Avoid starting things because he is afraid they will turn out badly anyway?
- Give up too quickly and too easily?
- Feel unhappy about his physical and sexual development?
- Dislike himself or put himself down?
- Feel he does not fit in or belong anywhere?
- Think no one loves him?
- Feel unlovable?

* * * * * *

- Seem to be losing interest in people and activities he had enjoyed?
- Have trouble making and keeping friends?
- Avoid people and social activities?
- Only like activities he can do alone?
- Refuse to talk to anyone about his feelings and thoughts?

Tries to Keep His Friends All to Himself

This sign can be caused by what may be a fact of human nature. It can be caused by jealousy, not having other friends, and the child's wanting to have what he has all to himself. Whatever the cause, it is a quick way for him to lose friends.

If a child is getting too possessive, his parents might say, for example, "I want to talk with you about you and your girlfriend. It's just something I learned along the way. Here it is. If you're too possessive, she might like it at first. After awhile, she'll want to spend time with her other friends and do stuff when you aren't around. This doesn't mean she doesn't still like you. It just means there's more to life than one relationship. Here's the problem. It works better not to be so possessive to begin with. I think if you keep it up, you might push her away. I have a couple of suggestions if you want to keep her as your girlfriend." Caution them to be careful, though. In all likelihood, the relationship will not last very long anyway. The risk is making him feel that breaking up was his fault whether his being too possessive had anything to do with it or not.

Often Gets His Feelings Hurt

This problem is not as simple as it may first seem. It looks like the child is just too thin-skinned and unable to handle the give-and-take of being ten or thirteen. It is a rough time and getting his feelings hurt happens easily if he lets it. This is just a fact of life for children, and for adults too, for that matter. The child's parents encouraging him to be a little tougher is normally good advice; but the sign may be a symptom of other problems.

Children with learning problems are more likely to get their feelings hurt by teachers and by other children. It hurts when people call attention to the youngster's not doing well, especially if he has tried to do well. Children whose self-esteem is already low feel even worse when things happen that other youngsters would not think much about one way or the other. Children who have high stress in their lives are much more vulnerable than those who do not. Handicapped youngsters, children with other physical or emotional problems, and those who are already self-conscious for some reason get their feelings hurt easily; and just being a child brings its own vulnerabilities. It really can be complicated for kids.

It is not enough for parents to encourage their child to be more thick-skinned. He needs help with his feelings and with how he thinks about himself. His parents can help here better than anyone since they are likely to be there when his feelings are hurting.

Encourage parents, at least at first, to take their child's side. They can start by getting a little angry for him about what happened and with whomever did it to him. He matters; and his feelings matter to his parents. He needs them on his side right now. Their advice and guidance can come later.

Often Becomes the Brunt of Teasing and Put-Downs

This sign of interpersonal maladjustment is usually caused by a combination of low self-esteem and poor social skills. Children who have good social skills and high self-esteem can handle the give-and-take. Usually, they either do not respond to the taunting or have developed ways of stopping it. Often this means using comebacks that are at least as nasty as the original taunt. Parents and other adults may object; but it works.

Parents' telling their child to ignore teasing and put-downs is good advice; but it only works up to a point and part of the time. Also, this does nothing to stop the assault on their child's self-esteem. Help them see that it is normally better for parents to stay out of it as much as they can. While they are staying on the sideline, encourage them to think about whether their child may be using this problem as a new way to get their attention. The point is that he needs to learn to deal with what is his problem.

A little coaching from his parents may help. He only needs to learn one or two social responses and use them calmly while looking the taunter straight in the eye. Whatever the taunter says next, he needs only to hold his ground, keep staring, and keep his mouth closed. If the child feels a need to say something, he might try, "Thank you for sharing that with me." If the taunter keeps it up, the social puzzle is just that much more challenging. He has to use the response every time for at least ten or fifteen tries, though. By that time, he has started to be socially proactive about his problems.

The strategy suggested assumes that the child is having his difficulties within a social context that includes other youngsters who are not exhibiting the more serious behavior disorders discussed in the last chapter. This means that his parents' first focus needs to be on with whom their child is having problems. They might first talk with school officials or others who have firsthand knowledge about the young people involved. If the youngsters involved are likely to exhibit abnormally extreme reactions to their child, have his parents explain to him that the taunters have serious behavior problems and that he should do whatever he can to avoid them. If that is not possible, the parents should talk with the people at school about how they should advise their child to handle the taunters' behavior.

Gets Uptight and Nervous When Anyone Is Angry or Upset

Getting a little uptight and nervous is normal, especially for a child. Even for adults, the situation brings some uncertainty. The uptightness is part of getting ready to deal with whatever happens. Nonetheless, if a child noticeably reacts like this with regularity, though, it signals a possible problem. This is especially true if he gets more upset than the person to whom he is reacting. If he has the reaction when the anger had nothing to do with him, it is a bigger problem. When he reacts just because he thinks someone might get angry, the problem is even worse.

What is happening? The child is overreacting. Why? Because he fears something very bad is about to happen, and probably to him. Children behave like they have learned to behave; and this is especially true for their emotional reactions. The child is afraid and fears he or someone else is going to get hurt.

Parents' helping their child with this sign is not complicated but takes a long time. Their child needs to learn that people get upset and angry at times; but this does not mean that someone is going to get hurt or that anything bad will happen. Encourage the youngster's parents to talk with him about his fears. They can say, "You feel upset. I think you're reacting to someone else's anger and nervousness. It feels like you're afraid that you or someone else might get hurt. It doesn't work that way in our family. (You need to help them be sure that this is true.) We all get angry at times. You can get angry too if something upsets you. Getting angry is okay. This is the difference. When we get angry, we talk to each other. Sometimes it gets a little loud; but that's as far as it goes. We don't hurt each other. You should let me know the next time you get angry about something. That is part of how we know what everyone in our family is thinking and feeling."

To again make and emphasize the point, his parents have to be sure that what they say is true. They must insist that no one hurts anyone at their house. This includes how the parents relate to each other, how they handle their anger and frustrations, and how they express their negative or unpleasant emotions. This again emphasizes the importance of parental modeling and the example they set for their children and the example their children set for each other.

Refuses to Stick Up for Himself

A child with this problem is well along the way to social isolation. In many ways, children who are having problems with fighting and getting into fights are getting along better than the child who just stands there and takes it. In the give-and-take, a child with this sign only takes. His parents may have taught him to be non-aggressive for religious or moral reasons; but if so, he will have a proud and self-controlled quality about him. The sign will be there; but it will not have a negative quality about it. A passive, "I have to take it," attitude is more likely. It is a whipped puppy kind of thing. The youngster is either afraid to stick up for himself or all the spunk has been taken out of him. Either way, it is a serious problem.

It is very difficult for parents to help their child with this sign. You can, nonetheless, have them do two things. First, they should try to get him to stick up for himself, especially in situations that have adult supervision. Next, when he does not stick up for himself at home, they should be slow to come to his aid. Home is a very good place for him to practice.

Here is the hard part for most parents. As the child exhibiting this sign begins to stick up for himself, he will likely use primitive methods. He may hit, yell, or try other things that are problematic. If so, they can say, for example, "You hit your sister. I'm proud of you for sticking up for yourself. You have the right idea; but hitting isn't your best choice. Next time, try just yelling at her. I don't know for sure if it'll work better. It's just something to think about."

Tries to Please Everyone and Keep Everyone Happy

This is a disguised version of a child's not sticking up for himself. As you encourage parents to think about it, they will see what motivates their child. On the surface, he wants approval, positive feedback, and to be seen as a helpful person who causes no trouble. The last part is the key. His main motivation is to cause no trouble. He wants to keep everyone from getting upset or angry, especially with him.

Instead of seeing the sign as the problem it is, many parents tend to see the behavior as positive, cooperative, and desirable; and in some ways, it is. The important question is how much and how often they see the behavior.

Trying to please everyone and keep everyone happy is likely the most common cause of tension and stress adults have. Ask parents with whom you are talking to think about themselves. How much of their stress is because of trying to meet everyone's needs and trying to keep everyone happy? They likely know it is unreasonable but may try to do it anyway. Help them see that they have an opportunity not to pass it on to their child.

This point needs your considered attention. The child learned what he was taught. Not pleasing adults or not keeping them happy may have lead to very bad things happening to him. It may have been his only hope for protecting himself. Even if there was no real threat, there may be an alcoholic or mentally ill family member for whom he feels responsible. The family law says, "Do whatever you have to do to avoid upsetting anyone. Keeping people happy is your job. If anyone gets upset, drinks, or gets mentally ill again, it's your fault." Guilt, especially irrational guilt, is powerful.

If none of the above conditions are present, have the child's parents discourage him from always doing things for people. They can be slower to let him help and tell him that it is not his job to keep people happy. In fact, he cannot make people happy and would be better off were he a little more selfish and self-centered. You can help his parents accept this concept, understanding that it probably will be difficult for them.

Feels Like Most People Do Not Like Him

Most children feel like this sometimes; and some feel this way most of the time. They really believe that most people do not like them. These feelings and ideas develop in children out of low self-esteem, bad life-experiences, poor social skills, and a life with way too much stress. Teach parents to focus on their having a positive relationship with their child, understanding that this helps a lot by itself. This truth not withstanding, they can do more to help their child with his interpersonal maladjustment issues.

They should start by believing him. They might say, "Okay, most people don't like you. I'm not one of those who doesn't like you; but most people are. If it's true, it must have something to do with how you act, how you look, or how you treat them. You must be turning them off. If we can figure out how you're doing that, we also can figure out how you can stop doing that. It's hard for me to see how you turn almost everyone off. That may be because I love you; but here's a place for us to start. How do they let you know they don't like you? That'll be a place for us to begin thinking about what you might do about the problem."

Is Rejected or Ignored by Most People His Age

This is the same as the last sign, except it is actually true: most people dislike the child. It is even worse if he does not understand that they do not like him.

His parents have to start by being honest with themselves and with their child. Their helping him starts with determining why he is so disliked. Since they are unlikely to have enough objectivity to see what others see, they might start by asking their child's teachers, other parents who they think would be candid with them or other adults who interact with their child. Also, they should not overlook the obvious. Other children have likely told their child why he is disliked. If they are patient, sensitive, and listen carefully, they will normally be able to learn the facts of it by asking him. With that information, they and he can work on changing or compensating for those characteristics that others find objectionable.

Worries and Frets About Not Doing Things Well Enough and About Failing

Parents may see this sign in relation to school and school work. Children get nervous and upset about tests, homework, and sometimes about going to school. The problem is that they think they will fail even when there is no reason for them to worry. They do not do their homework, will not participate in class, and do not risk failure. Sometimes a child with self-esteem problems will do his homework but not turn it in. The risk of teachers and parents getting upset is not as bad as failing.

This type of self-esteem problem also may be seen in other areas. The young person worries and frets about not looking good enough and may even think he looks weird. He may avoid other children because he is afraid of being embarrassed. He thinks he will fail socially or may think that he already is a social failure. New people and activities are always a problem because he does not know what new ways there might be to embarrass himself or to fail. He thinks that almost anything or anyone may be a new chance for him to be rejected.

What is going on with the child? It is one of those things that is so obvious parents can completely overlook it. Yes, it has to do with how the youngster thinks about and feels about himself. More importantly, though, it has to do with how he thinks others feel about him, how he thinks they will react to him. Children with low self-esteem believe that people do not like them and that they will never be accepted.

Is a child with low self-esteem worrying and fretting about not doing well and about failing? Yes; but more to the point, he worries more about ridicule, rejection, and angry reactions. If this were not bad enough, he knows it would be still worse to just be ignored.

A couple things will be helpful for parents. Problems with low self-esteem are very stressful for children. For example, worrying and fretting once in a while about failing is not all that significant. All children do this sometimes. Still, some kids often feel like this; and for them, their stress is severe. When parents frequently see this behavior in their child, they need to be alert to signs of stress and look for times when they can back off a little and reduce the pressure on him to work harder or do more.

When their child is working on something or thinking about doing something, be sure they resist the temptation to say things to him like, "Don't worry. You'll do fine. You're getting upset over nothing." This only says to him that they do not understand how upset and afraid he really is.

It would be better for them to say, "I'm proud of you for taking a chance on yourself. I think it will work out fine but don't know for sure. I just want you to know I'm here for you no matter how it turns out. Your being willing to try or at least thinking about it tells me you are my kind of person."

The child's parents' goal is to find within themselves enough patience and sensitivity to first try understanding and then supporting their child's struggle. Their support needs to be there for him however it turns out. He is important to them; and knowing that he belongs and is accepted by his parents boosts his self-esteem all by itself.

When their child does take a chance and try, his parents need to actively acknowledge the good points about what he does. At the same time, they must not be dishonest. They should not say that he did well when it is not true, tell him things are going fine when they are not, or try to convince him that people like him when they do not. Most importantly, they must resist the natural temptation to tell him that it does not matter because it does matter. They and he both know it matters a lot.

This is the question parents may need to answer. Do they have enough respect and caring for their child to be honest? For him to know they do is a very positive and loving thing. Within the love and honesty of their relationship, they can authenticly encourage him, support him, give him ideas about how he can succeed, and be there for him when things go sour.

Resists Starting Things Because He Is Afraid They Will Turn Out Badly Anyway

Worrying and fretting is where low self-esteem starts. Just shutting down is where it leads. This is the first hurdle to help parents get over. Children whose self-esteem is so low they will not even try are misunderstood and often dealt with in harsh and destructive ways. Parents may see them as bull-headed, oppositional, and defiant. Their child's self-esteem problem looks to them like a behavior problem. From that perspective, they can quickly become frustrated, angry, and down on their child. It is a vicious circle. The child does not try to do things because he believes he will fail anyway. He thinks he will get bad reactions from people no matter how he does. His parents see his behavior as willful and defiant. They get upset and angry with him which is what he thought they were going to do. It makes no difference. Bad reactions and rejection come anyway. From the child's point of view, he is simply someone to whom others react badly; and he does not have to do anything to get the bad reactions. As the saying goes, "Damned if he does and damned if he doesn't;" so why should he bother?

Teach the child's parents to interpret his behavior in literal terms. He does not start projects or try new things, makes no effort to participate, and always has excuses such as "I forgot."

Managing this behavior is difficult; but nonetheless, advise parents to use this approach. Their first goal is to get their child to start or at least try, not to get him to finish or do well. Any effort he makes is a very big step in the right direction. Trying one problem, at least going to the activity, or making a little effort to do what they expect is progress.

They must not get angry or frustrated with him; for if they do, they would have done better by doing nothing. The same holds for threatening and pleading with him. A better approach is to offer him something he wants if he will just start and at least try. This might be a small privilege, a special treat, time doing something fun with them, or anything else he values.

Gives Up Too Quickly and Too Easily

A child with low self-esteem worries and frets about failing. He starts giving up quicker and easier. Finally, he just does not try. When the child is giving up too quickly and too easily, he is on his way to shutting down, although occasionally, giving up quickly is the last step and comes after not starting or trying.

Here is how it works. Fretting and worrying changed to giving up quickly and easily. Criticism and angry reactions from parents, other adults, or peers caused the youngster to give up. At some point, he just quit.

The child asked himself, "What can I do?" This was his answer. "Just go through the motions. Act like you're trying. Stop as soon as they get off your back." The child is not trying to succeed; he is only trying to keep things from getting worse. He does not want to be put down and hurt.

The young person needs to know that his parents love him for who he is and not for how well he does. His parents need to accept him on an as-is basis. They should respond positively anytime he makes an effort of any kind to please, especially when he is trying to please them.

Persistently Feels Very Unhappy About his Physical and Sexual Development

Low self-esteem starts with worrying and fretting about failing. It grows into giving up quickly. This leads to shutting down and not trying. If parental or other adult reactions are too harsh, the child goes through the motions for fear of even harsher consequences. He simply plays the game. This is a very sad way for him to think and feel about success, achievement, and interpersonal participation. Nonetheless, low self-esteem can get still worse for him.

The youngster feels incompetent and may have a low physical/sexual self-image as well. Most children have some uncertainty about themselves physically and sexually; but children with self-esteem problems have these thoughts persistently and feel them strongly. They think they cannot succeed, cannot achieve, and that they will not be accepted socially. They also may think that they are not made right or well enough.

This poor self-image has nothing to do with how the young person actually looks or is developing. The child believes it, no matter what the facts are or what his parents tell him.

Caution his parents to resist trying to convince him that his perceptions and feelings are wrong. That will only strengthen his belief that they do not understand. They can say, "I feel badly you think about yourself in such negative ways. You're a normal person and are fine physically and sexually. I know you doubt that even though it is true. I want to hear what you think and feel about it; but I'm not going to argue. You have a right to your feelings. Will you tell me how it feels to you?"

Dislikes Himself or Puts Himself Down

This sign makes the child's physical and sexual doubt easier to understand. It also makes it easier to see the connection between low self-esteem and interpersonal maladjustment. Children believe they are who parents and other people have told them they are. The messages may have come directly from their parents or perhaps from teachers or peers. Wherever they came from, it was a part of the child's world that did not value and support him.

It is as if he steps back, watches himself, and hears people saying to him, "You aren't someone I like. You aren't my kind of person. There're a lot of things I don't like about you; and I'm here to point them out to you, every chance I get." The youngster learned to watch himself by having to live through what others said to him and about him to others. He painfully saw how they saw him and how they treated him.

There is no way the young person's parents can directly help with this kind of self-hatred. Saying, "I love you," is worth saying but does not help much. Mostly, it makes the child think that they are as dumb as he feels. They are just someone else who lies to him.

Instead, the child needs his parents to actively value and care. He needs that relationship to be certain, secure, and authentic. Though it may be difficult for them, try to focus their thinking on the relationship itself and away from behavior and specific events. The quality of their relationship with their child is the heart of the message he needs from them. It needs to consistently say, "You're someone worth my hanging in there with. I'm part of you as you are of me. We go together. However steep the hill and no matter how long it takes, we'll climb it together."

In the short term, have the child's parents listen for a couple days and make note of the bad things he says about himself. Have them then find a quiet time to talk with him about their list. If possible and if both of his parents are available, they should talk with him together since he needs to know that they both care and are together with him on this. They can say, "For the last two days, we've made a note every time we heard you put yourself down. Here's the list of things you've said about yourself." They should then quietly read the list to him and wait for a minute to see if he says anything.

Next, they can say, "We don't see you like that. These things don't seem like you to us. We'd like to get you to help us understand. If it's okay with you, we'll read these to you one at a time. We'd like for you to tell us why you think these things are true about you. You may want to give us an example or just explain it to us. The first thing on the list is, 'I just mess everything up.' Why do you believe that is true? Will you give us an example?"

This is critical. They must not argue with him, must not try to convince him that he is wrong. They should simply ask questions and listen. That by itself lets him know that they care and value what he has to say. Once they have listened to what he feels about each put-down, they can say, "Thank you for sharing your thoughts and feelings with us. We understand how you see yourself a lot better. We don't see you in those ways at all but appreciate your being willing to help us understand."

The conversation helped the youngster's self-esteem all by itself. Also, they now have many new opportunities. Suppose their family goes to church and then to visit with some friends; and things go fine. Later that night, they can make a point to talk with their child. They might say, "Remember when you said you mess everything up? Well, today was an example of why we don't agree. Today was a very good day. Everything went fine. It was good to have you with us. You didn't mess anything up. That makes us think you're not someone who messes everything up. We just want you to know why we think what we think." The child likely will not say anything. They have made their self-esteem point nonetheless.

Feels He Does Not Fit In or Belong Anywhere

This is the underlying problem causing the child's low self-esteem. He feels like he does not fit in, does not belong. This goes against what may be the most human of human needs: the need to belong. Children are who others tell them they are; and youngsters with very low self-esteem have heard their world telling them that they do not belong anywhere. They think they do not fit in, do not belong. As sad as it is, they are partly right. Whether it is at home or somewhere else, to some extent they do not fit in or belong in what is to them an important part of their world.

This makes parents' helping their child with his self-esteem problems doubly difficult. They need to help him with his ideas about himself that are not true as well as with those that are true.

For example, their child says, "I don't belong anywhere. No one cares about me." Encourage his parents to say, "You belong here and I care about you; but you think that is not true. I don't understand why you feel that way. That doesn't help you much right now. I feel badly for you but am not going to tell you how to feel or what to think. I'm here for you and hope that helps at least a little. I hope you will hang in there with me and keep trying to help me understand why you don't feel like you belong and why you don't think I care." The idea is to help them actively value and respect their child enough to deal with the truth, with how he really feels.

Thinks No One Loves Him

This sign is one step down the self-esteem ladder from perceptions of not fitting in and not belonging. It is almost all the way to the bottom.

When you are talking with parents about their child's problems, there are a couple points to consider. Most children and most adults for that matter sometimes feel unloved and unappreciated; and many feel a little like this much of the time. Their feelings may be about low self-esteem; but they are more likely because of some atypical circumstance. When feeling unloved is a sign of damaged self-esteem, it is much more constant, much more severe, and very painful.

The child says, "No one loves me. No one cares." His parents likely are tempted to say, "I love you. I care." It is important for them to then go on to say, "Not feeling loved is a hard feeling to handle. I can tell it feels awful and hurts a lot. It seems like you feel angry and afraid and other confusing stuff at the same time. Not thinking anyone cares would feel really lonely. How does it feel to you?" At least the child now knows that they care enough to care about how he feels. That is a start.

"I love you's" are cheap; but when parents are gentle and honest, their child learns that he matters enough to be listened to. This is a small bit of self-esteem, a moment when important people in his life respect him enough to deal with him openly and honestly.

Feels Unlovable

This is the bottom of the self-esteem ladder. The child has totally devalued himself and sees himself as a zero. He has given up.

Have parents think about how the child's loss of self-esteem progressed. It went from worrying and fretting to giving up too easily, from not trying to self-hatred. The child now is at the end of the line. From his point of view, he has no value, is not someone anyone loves. Why? Because he is simply not lovable. People may say that they care and may even pretend to love him; but it is not possible for anyone to love him. He is not someone anyone should love. When a child's self-esteem has been this permanently destroyed, the child has a lifelong disability. It is something from which he can never fully recover.

Your best strategy is to be sure his parents take full advantage of any opportunity they may have to actively value him, support him, and increase his sense of belonging and attachment to them and to other positive people who care.

- Each gentle touch makes life slightly less bad for him.
- Each quiet moment gives him a small taste of belonging.
- Each time his parents listen says he matters a little.
- Each time they are sensitive and patient, he is a little less handicapped.

Losing Interest in Most People and Activities

This is a sign of withdrawal. Help parents think about this sign carefully and not be too quick to think there is a problem. Their child may lose interest in some people and some activities but this usually has nothing to do with withdrawal. Perhaps he became bored or simply got interested in other things. This sign is more than simply changing his interests.

The child's parents need to watch to see if the people and activities in which he is losing interest are being replaced by other people and activities. If so, a problem is unlikely. If not, their child may be withdrawing. Encourage his parents to talk with him about what they have noticed. They can say, "I've been noticing you're withdrawing from people and activities. It isn't just changing interests. For example (Give some examples), you stay by yourself and don't seem interested in much. Will you help me understand what's happening?"

He may tell them that he is into his school work and does not have time for activities. If so, they should say, "School work is okay but a steady diet of it is too much. I think there is more happening. Talk to me about what happened with your friends and with the activities you had enjoyed." If they are patient and give it a little time, he will likely tell them what happened in his world to cause things to go sour.

Trouble Making and Keeping Friends

Some children are more likely to exhibit this sign of interpersonal maladjustment than others. For example, if a child has changed neighborhoods and schools, difficulty making and keeping friends is more likely; or if his life-experiences have not taught him good interpersonal and relationship skills, having the problem is nearly inevitable. A child who has low self-esteem and deals less well with the give-and-take of friends and the social scene will have this problem to some degree.

Most children move out from a solid base at home into other relationships, enabling them to try many relationships while always having those at home. Children who do not have this solid base will certainly have this problem. Because of this, relationships they do find are more important to them. For example, they can easily become too possessive and smother the other person; or they may try too hard to please and to be part of the group, making them very vulnerable to mistreatment and exploitation.

Their child needs to be taught about friends and relationships. Have his parents approach their teaching task like this: "Getting a friend starts by hanging around with people who are like you want to be. Pick people who seem to value what you value. Next, talk and join in without being pushy. After a while, you'll notice you talk more with some of them than others. There'll be two or three you talk with the most. You and they are becoming friends. There're also some ways to keep friends and ways that turn them off. We can talk about that as time goes on." By talking to him like this, they are modeling an example of friendly behavior and are teaching him relationship skills. Parents will need your support to understand that it is a slow but rewarding process.

Be sure they also make a point to include him in family activities at church, in the neighborhood, or in community organizations. This gives him a chance to see other healthy families and to make friends. Although child-only activities may be too stressful for him at first, family activities are safe and provide his parents an opportunity to observe, coach, and support him.

Avoids People and Social Activities

This is a sign that the child has withdrawn. Parents could easily miss it because their child may be very friendly with them, with other family members, and especially with adults. His parents say, "But everyone likes him." The problem is that "everyone" includes few if any young people his age.

If their child has really withdrawn from everyone, he needs immediate psychiatric help. Something drastic is happening. If the withdrawal is from other children and activities away from home, it is serious but not so much of an emergency. He still has his parents and others in his family.

His parents should try two things. First, talk with him about what is going on. He may tell them what is happening and what he thinks and feels. This will give them clues about how to help. Next, they need to back off a little from being his best friend. His parent is the only mother (or father) he has. That is their job. If a parent is his main friend, it keeps him from needing to find other friends.

His parents should facilitate his spending more time around young people his age. They may need to push and insist a little. The best technique is to stay close but give him room to be with other children.

Only Likes Activities He Can Do Alone

This can be near the end of the withdrawal road. This sign also may be seen in a child who never developed satisfying relationships with people. These children have their most significant relationships with things and may be known as bookworms or, these days, computer nuts. Their only interest might be music, reading, television, or anything else where they do not have to deal with people.

Helping parents be clear about their goal is the key to helping their child. Their goal is not to get him to where he prefers people to his books and computers but rather only to get him to be a little more socially active.

As with most signs of maladjustment, parents' helping starts with their relationship with their child. Teach them to show more interest in what he has read, in what he has learned to make his computer do, or in what he is watching on television. When he responds a little to their interest, they should feel good about his progress. It will additionally help for his parents to encourage him to tell others about his interests.

If his parents try increasing the time he spends with other children, be sure they do not make what is a very common mistake. People often try to match a withdrawn child with one who is unusually outgoing. A better match would be with a child who is almost as quiet and reserved as the withdrawn youngster. No, they will not bore each other to death. They also will not overwhelm each other.

Refuses to Talk to Anyone About His Feelings and Thoughts

Typically, the presence of this sign is because the child feels like no one listens or seems to care about what he thinks and feels. Even worse, those who act like they cared do nothing but tell him what he should think and how he should feel. He tried telling them what he thought. They said things like, "You don't really believe that do you?" "That's a stupid thing to think." "You shouldn't feel that way."

Does he see things this way at his house? Asking him is a place for his parents to start. When they ask him, they need to be sure that they are ready for the answer. Their getting upset or telling him he is wrong will only prove to him that he is not wrong.

Teach the child's parents to ask him questions about day-to-day things and show him that they are interested in him, what he thinks, and how he feels.

The youngster's parents should not push him to talk. His relationship with them should be on his terms. They can talk to him about day-to-day kinds of things but should not expect him to respond. They are there and interested and accept the reality that he will talk to them when he wants to talk. In the meantime, they can offer to play games and do things where he does not need to talk.

CHAPTER 7

MENTAL ILLNESS

Overview

Mental illness is many things. Like physical illness, mental illness can affect anyone and has many forms. The first important point to help parents understand is that mental illness is not just one illness but is many illnesses.

It will help for them to think about it in this way. There is the part of the child that thinks and understands. They can call this part the child's mind. There is the part that feels happy and sad, frightened and calm, angry and joyful. They can call this part the emotions. Also there is the part that does things and takes action based on what the youngster thinks and feels. They can call this part behavior.

What is mental illness? The child's mind, emotions, and behavior normally work together as a team. When children become mentally ill, the three members of the team stop working together. They each start functioning independent of each other and the child cannot get them to start working together again.

Some kinds of mental illness affect the mind the most. The youngster is unable to think clearly and understand things the way they really are. The world becomes a strange and confusing place for him.

Other kinds of mental illness affect emotions more and other kinds affect behavior more; but all types of mental illness affect the child's mind, emotions, and behavior to some extent and in some way. When this happens, the young person finds it very hard to keep the three members of the team under control and working together. Help parents to keep this problem of teamwork in mind as they think about whether their child may be mentally ill.

Signs of Mental Illness

For the most part, children who are not mentally ill never exhibit these signs. If parents notice any of these signs in their child, the first step is to talk with their family physician about what they have observed. Their physician will probably suggest that they have their child evaluated by a children's mental health specialist. Emphasize with them the importance of following whatever recommendations they receive.

Think with the child's parents about these questions. They highlight common signs of mental illness. As they consider each question, have them ask themselves if their child ever exhibits the sign. If not, they should go to the next question. If he sometimes has the problem, put a check mark beside the question and then go to the next question. Step them through the questions until they have thought about each question.

Does Their Child:

- Have extreme mood swings? (His mood jumps from one extreme to the other and he cannot control it.)
- Vomit after eating or use laxatives to control his weight?
- Go on extreme eating binges? (May or may not be unusually overweight.)
- Starve himself?
- Distrust everyone and think people are out to get him?
- Have very strange thoughts and feelings he cannot understand or control?
- Have extreme fears that keep him from doing things most people the same age do easily?
- Get extremely uncomfortable if someone gets close or touches him?
- Urinate or defecate in his clothes? (This applies to children over eight or nine-years-old and does not include wetting the bed.)
- Cut or hurt himself on purpose?
- Have an unusual interest in fire, watching fires, setting fires, and doing things with fire?
- Hear voices and see things others do not hear and cannot see?

Mood Jumps from One Extreme to the Other and He Cannot Control It

There are several reasons why it might be difficult for a child to control his mood and emotions. Two of the most likely are being upset and excitement. The child becomes upset or excited and his emotions get a little out of hand. Nonetheless, he normally can settle down if necessary, at least for a few minutes. With this sign, his mood jumping to the extremes needs to be combined with an inability to control it before the behavior is significant.

A potential cause of the sign is depression. A depressed child often does not behave like his parents expect. They might think he would be in a down mood and not very active. His depression may look like this but is just as likely to look quite differently.

One aspect of depression in children fits this sign well. The child's moods and emotions flip around unpredictably. For example, he may be very up and have a lot of energy and then down and withdrawn, open and friendly and then very angry for no reason his parents can see. The important thing is for them to see that he cannot stop the emotional turmoil by himself and needs specialized help with his depression.

Another cause of this sign is serious mental illness. If this is what is happening with their child, his parents would likely see one or more of the other signs discussed in this chapter.

Here is what you need to emphasize with the child's parents: Arguing and getting upset with their child only makes things worse. It is not a problem that has anything to do with discipline or willfulness. The youngster's emotions and reactions really are out of control; and he cannot help it. Patience and tolerance are in order along with a careful evaluation by their family physician. If this evaluation does not result in a referral to a children's mental health specialist, you should discuss with the child's parents the possibility of their getting a second opinion.

Vomits After Eating or Uses Laxatives to Control His Weight

Vomiting after eating is most likely caused by a minor illness or intestinal problem. With any sign, a physical problem may be all or part of the cause. The child is much more likely to be physically ill than mentally ill.

When vomiting or laxatives are being used by the child to control his weight, he has a serious problem.[27] He may have thought of it by himself or may have picked the idea up from a friend or something he read. The

[27]Youngsters in athletic activities such as gymnastics or wrestling are particularly susceptible to this behavior, given the emphasis on weight control.

point is that the behavior is dangerous and is both physically and psychologically unhealthy.

The behavior is common enough that parents need to watch for it whether they suspect the problem or not. They should watch for:

- Their child's needing to use the bathroom immediately after or during meals.
- Unpleasant or unusual odors in the bathroom or other rooms in their house.
- Any hints or clues when he talks with them or with his friends.
- Unusual body odor or bad breath.
- Gray or darkening teeth.

Here is the point you need to stress with parents. The behavior can cause permanent physical damage and even their child's death, if it goes to the extreme. They must talk with him about the problem even if they do not think he has it. Talking about it will not give him the idea but will teach him about the dangers so he is aware of them when he hears about the behavior at school or somewhere else.

If the young person's parents suspect that he is or may be involved in the behavior, they need to talk with him. Also, they must closely watch him for a couple of weeks; and if their concerns are not satisfied, they need to get him to a children's eating disorder specialist. They and he cannot handle this problem by themselves. Even if the behavior seems to stop, his parents should keep an eye out. It is likely to start back up.

Goes on Extreme Eating Binges

Like other signs of mental illness, this sign can have several causes. One likely cause is depression combined with the child's nervousness and uptightness. Eating is something to do and a way of dealing with his nervous energy. Eating far too much is somewhat like a natural tranquilizer that makes the young person a little drowsy and calmer.

Another cause is part of an eating disorder called bulimia and is related to the last sign. The child's weight likely is about right for his height and age; but nonetheless, he vomits to control his weight. After eating, he purges or gets rid of what he has just eaten. As if trying to make up for the purging, he eats huge amounts of food in one sitting. This is not just overeating. In one sitting, the child may eat enough food to serve as normal meals for ten or twenty people. Keeping food away from him or locking up the food usually does little good and may make matters worse. The youngster needs specialized help immediately.

Starves Himself

First, make this point with parents. Dieting is never a good idea for a child under twelve or thirteen, unless directly supervised by a physician. Even a day or so of eating little to nothing is dangerous for preadolescent children. While the child's food is severely restricted, he does not grow. Even worse, he may never make up for the time he was not growing. This is very serious. A young child should never diet unless medically supervised. It is as simple as that.

For a teenager, watching his weight is usually not a problem, although his parents' checking with a physician is a good idea. Even an adolescent's eating little to nothing for a day or two once in a while usually does not hurt anything; but his parents must be sure that the dieting is not extreme. Further, they need to be sure it does not go on for more than a couple days at a time and does not happen more than once in a while. If the child has a weight problem, arranging for him to talk with his physician is the place for his parents to start.

This sign is part of an eating disorder called anorexia and has little to do with dieting or normal weight control. A child exhibiting this sign is starving himself. The first thing his parents would notice is his losing weight. Next, they would notice his getting thin and that he is eating little to nothing. He might tell them that he is watching his weight, is not hungry, or does not feel well. Whatever his reason is, he is not eating enough.

Here is the hard part for most parents to understand. Even though their child is already thin, he thinks he is fat or at least thinks he is overweight. How he looks to his parents does not fit with his perception of himself. His self-perception is distorted or does not fit with how he really is. He has lost his ability to judge himself and feels fat no matter what the truth is.

When parents see this sign in their child, his need for specialized help is urgent. They nor their child can handle the problem without help. You may be able to get them to go for help quicker if you explain to them that their child can die from the behavior. It does have to do with depression and low self-esteem; but it is much more complicated. Specialized care is always necessary.

Mistrusts Everyone and Thinks People Are Out to Get Him

Whether parents should be concerned about this sign is a matter of how strongly and how often they see the sign. Also, encourage them to consider how they might feel were they their child. Maybe people actually are not to be trusted and are out to get him. Their child may be right.

It is not unusual for a child to feel used sometimes and to be somewhat leery of people. It becomes a problem when he starts changing what he does or does not do, where he will and will not go. It is a problem when it interferes with his normal, day-to-day activities. The problem gets worse when the youngster thinks people are trying to hurt him and more so if he is not sure who "they" are or if "they" are not people who are likely to hurt him. For example, he might come to believe most teachers or perhaps his parents are trying to control his mind or find a chance to kill him.

Here is the question you should raise with the child's parents. Are their child's fears far beyond anything real, beyond reason, or quite weird? If so, he likely has a very serious mental illness-related problem and needs psychiatric help.

Very Strange Thoughts and Feelings He Cannot Understand or Control

Any child may need help understanding his thoughts and feelings. At times, he may need extra understanding from his parents and time to talk about what is going on in his life. His thoughts and feelings may seem strange to him and be hard for him to figure out; but his parents may see them as little more than a part of growing up.

There are two things that should cause the child's parents concern, though. If their child's thoughts and feelings make him very uneasy and do not go away in a couple of weeks, counseling likely will help. Also, if they make his parents very uncomfortable, their talking with the child's physician is wise. If the thoughts and feelings are violent or destructive, it is a sign of anger and rage and is something the child needs help with right away.

If a child's thoughts and beliefs are quite strange or very out of the ordinary, specialized mental health intervention is important. These kinds of thoughts and ideas might include the child's thinking that he has special powers, that people are controlling his thoughts, or other supernatural or far-out beliefs. His parents need to take time to be sure that he is not just pretending or putting them on. Nonetheless, strange and uncontrolled thoughts and feelings can be a sign of serious mental illness.

Extreme Fears that Keep Him from Doing Things Most Children His Age Do Easily

Fear is a feeling every child has from time-to-time. Normal fears can be very strong and make it hard for the child to handle the give-and-take of his days and weeks. Still, these fears do not keep him from doing the kinds of things most children do. At the rough points, a little understanding from his parents and a good pep talk are enough to get him to get on with getting on.

Two types of fear are very serious, though. The first is fear of separating from home and important adults. The second is less specific. It ranges from being afraid of some things and situations to being afraid most of the time.

Fear of separating is called separation anxiety. This is often seen as a fear of going to school but comes up sometimes as a fear of being alone or of being left. Being afraid to go to school is interesting. It looks like the child is afraid of going to school. There may be a good reason to be afraid of something at school; but his parents need to be cautious about coming to the conclusion that the problem is at school. Usually, school is not something children have any good reason to fear. The truth likely is that he does not want to be away from home and fears the separation. Your advice should be for the youngster's parents to get professional help for him. If he gets quick, specialized help, three or four weeks of behavior therapy usually corrects the problem.

For his parents' part, the main thing will be to calmly but firmly make him go to school. They should take him if that is the only way to get him to go.

Once in a while, a child develops extreme and very puzzling fears. What start out as normal fears get so strong that they keep the child from doing normal kinds of things. Perhaps the child may start being afraid of things that are not real. He might fear odd things like becoming invisible, turning into a horse, being killed by rays from outer space, or something else just as weird. These fears are likely signs of mental illness and need assessed by a children's mental health specialist.

Trouble Having People Close or Touching Him

This sign has to be extreme to be important. When it is, the child is mentally ill and needs long-term treatment.[28]

Here is what parents need to know. Usually, their child will be comfortable with touching, hugging, and having people close to him. By eight or ten, he may like less of this type of attention, especially from his parents. They will notice a lot of difference from child to child; and a specific child may like this kind of attention some days and not others.

Whether their child holds back or wants to be touched, when touching him or initiating physical contact, his parents should ask themselves this. "Does he really want to do this?" Unless they are sure he does, they need to take it very slowly and gently. The best approach to suggest is for them to stay close but let their child control the touching, especially when it is a gesture of affection or just playful. He is the one to decide about touching and who touches him.

The best practice for them is to ask, "Would you like a hug?" "May I put my arm around you?" "May I look at the bruise on your leg?" While they are still outside his room and without opening his door, his parents can ask, "May I come in to talk a minute?" If he says that they cannot, they should respect his wishes.

Urinates or Defecates in His Clothes

This is usually a serious problem sometimes caused by medical difficulties but more often by emotional troubles. Keep in mind that a child ten or twelve-years-old sometimes might have an accident. Even so, it is unlikely for children that old. If parents see the sign in their child, a physical examination is necessary. A real physical problem may be the cause.

Here are a couple of things to be sure parents know. Even if the problem is emotional, it can become physical if it goes on too long. Not regularly going to the bathroom causes physical problems. This means the child needs medical care for the problem, even if the etiology is emotional.

There is not much parents can do to help except calmly have their

---

[28]Not wanting to be touched or have people physically close may be an indication of child neglect on the one hand or abuse on the other, but usually is not. Especially when the aversion is to everyone, underlying mental illness is likely.

child clean himself each time he has trouble. Making any more of it will only make his problem worse.

It is specifically important for parents with whom you talk about toilet-related problems to separate bed-wetting from other difficulties and not attribute undue seriousness to problems exhibited by kids under six or seven. Bed-wetting sometimes follows from parent to child and has a genetic component. A small percentage of teens are bed-wetters and do not have any significant problems. If parents are concerned, they should consult with a pediatrician about their child's behavior.

Cuts and Hurts Himself on Purpose

A child might cut or hurt himself and really just be fooling around; but it is unlikely. Even then, it will happen once or twice and stop. If the cut or injury is more than minor or if the behavior persists, the child has a problem.

His parents talking with him about the behavior and listening carefully for other signs of maladjustment will help. This is a very serious problem; and if it happens more than once or twice, the young person needs a mental health evaluation. Also, his parents should look very closely for other signs they may have overlooked. With emphasis, be sure they do not accept the explanation they may receive from others that he is doing it for attention. It is much more serious than that.[29]

Although self-mutilating behavior is most likely related to mental illness, it may have other origins. For example, the behavior may be related to gang initiation activities or may be a fad in which youngsters in an area are participating. Whatever the etiology, parents need to pursue the behavior until they understand the "why" of it and until it stops.

A Persistent Interest in Fire, Watching Fires, Setting Fires, and Doing Things with Fire

A child might like to build fires and watch a fire burning. At the same time, he understands the danger and is careful. Also, fire is not something he thinks about much.

---

[29]A school principal saw "scratches" on a young boy's wrists. The child said he was trying to kill himself but was not believed. The "hesitation marks" were dismissed as attention seeking behavior instead of being recognized as indicators of intentional, self-mutilating behavior associated with underlying emotional illness. The child drowned himself two days later.

A child who has a problem with fire has a much different set of thoughts and feelings about fire. He thinks a lot about it and looks for chances to set fires, to watch fires, and to do things with fire.

Before ten or so, the child's playing with matches or lighters may cause a fire or get parents concerned in other ways; but typically, this is a behavior problem and not a sign of mental illness. By ten to twelve, though, it is more than a behavior problem, although a simple accident can still happen.

If their child has a problem with fire, his parents can invest some effort in keeping matches and lighters away from him and to take time to teach him safe use of matches and fire. Also, talking with a fireman might have some educational value. Nonetheless, these activities should not be used to frighten or scare their child. It is likely that he has other problems that may be less easy to see.

Here is the important point to emphasize with the child's parents. Getting angry with him or punishing him are likely only to make his problems worse. For example, he may become more secretive, more clever at hiding the behavior, and even more fascinated. Certainly, talking is important as is a warm, safe family environment. Even so, specialized help is necessary.

Hears Voices and Sees Things Others Do not Hear and Cannot See

This sign is called hallucinating and can be caused by high fevers, drug reactions, or some type of poisoning. If the sign suddenly appears, parents must consider these possibilities first. They mean that their child needs medical attention immediately.

A child may tell his parents about things that may seem like auditory or visual hallucinations when they are only dreams. At other times, it just seems to him like something odd happened when it did not. Any of these causes do not last long and do not recur. Even at that, parents should not just brush them off as unimportant. As with other signs, they should watch for additional indicators of difficulty.

When hallucinations are a sign of mental illness, they will happen from time to time. Also, the child believes they are real. Usually, he will tell his parents about them, especially if they ask if he is still hearing the voices or seeing the visions. If not, they can likely tell by watching him.They will see he is watching the visions or listening to the voices.

Let's finish consideration of mentally ill children by making this point one more time. These signs are very serious. If parents see any of them in their child, it is critical for them to get specialized help. Their physician will help them get the help their child must have.

CHAPTER 8

COMMON MEDICAL CONCERNS

Overview

As you talk with parents about their children, they will occasionally mention problems that may need medical attention. Of course, if a child's parents ask you if they should consult with a physician about a concern they are having, you should always advise them to do so. Unless you are a physician or have been specifically medically trained, a medical referral is, without exception, your best choice whenever a problem may be medically related. This especially applies to reports of signs, symptoms, or problems that seem unusual, severe, or about which you have no knowledge or information.

Below are common signs of medical difficulties you may want to explore with parents or about which comments or questions may come up in your discussions. Each of the listed signs needs medically evaluated[30] and some mean that there is an emergency. The additional comments accompanying a few of the signs will assist parents with whom you are talking to better understand the specific signs.

Signs Needing Medical Attention

- Vomiting, especially if it recurs and does not completely stop within six hours or if there are more than minor streaks or traces of blood in the vomited material.
- Difficulty swallowing.
- Frequent or severe stomachaches, especially if they awaken the child during the night or are localized in specific areas (other than the navel).
- A rash that persists for more than four or five days or is accompanied by a fever or sore throat.

[30]Most physicians will either personally consult with parents by phone or have a nurse or other assistant available to consult by phone. This service allows parents to discuss their child's problem(s) with a medical professional before deciding whether to schedule an appointment. There is usually no charge for this service.

- Frequent wheezing. Be sure that parents understand that wheezing may seem to them to have stopped but continue to be a problem that only trained medical personnel can detect.
- Frequent coughing not obviously related to a cold or persisting for more than three or four days.
- Diarrhea, i.e., watery stool occurring more than four or five times in a day, especially if it lasts for more than one or two days or if there are several watery stools per hour over five or six hours.
- Difficulty seeing, using one eye more than the other, frequent squinting, blurred vision, or double vision. Blurred or double vision should be treated as a medical emergency.
- Frequent or severe earaches. Do not apply heat to an earache. Instead, a cold compress should be used. (Be sure parents understand that some drainage of wax from the ear is likely not significant but that discharge or drainage of milky or greenish matter needs medical attention.)
- Ringing sensations or fullness in the ears, especially if the discomfort, ringing, or fullness lasts for more than a day or two.
- Difficulty hearing, especially if it persists.
- Bleeding, especially from the ears, eyes, mouth, or bleeding that will not stop within five to six minutes or does not begin to slow in three minutes or so.
- An elevated temperature, especially if it lasts for more than a day or goes over 101 degrees. Be sure that parents understand that an elevated temperature is not necessarily serious but normally should be reported to the child's physician.
- A sore throat lasting for more than a day or two or if there is swelling or problems swallowing. It is usually even more significant if a child with a sore throat also has a fever.
- Red, runny, or swollen eyes. This is usually not a sign that there is an immediate threat to the child's health but does need evaluated to determine the significance of the symptoms. If parents suspect that there may be something in the child's eye and the symptoms do not clear in fifteen minutes or so, consulting with a physician is necessary.
- Frequent or severe headaches, including headaches that last for more than a few hours *no matter how severe* or headaches associated with vomiting.

- Stuttering, stammering, or incoherent speech, especially if the problem persists or is not obviously related to excitement or other strong emotions.
- A bluish tinge to lips (including the tongue or the inside of the mouth), ear lobes, or fingernails, especially when unrelated to being cold. If the symptoms suddenly appear, consult with a physician immediately.
- Shortness of breath or wheezing after slight exertion, especially if the sign recurs.
- Pain or burning when urinating. Also watch for more than traces of blood in the stool or any blood in the urine.
- Persistent itching, pain, sores, a rash or other irritation, or more than slight and temporary discomfort in the genital or rectal area.
- Cuts, scratches, or bruises that do not heal noticeably in a few days. Also watch for any unusual, multiple, or severe bruises, scars, burns, or other injuries not obviously related to trauma or in unusual places such as the back.
- Swollen joints or swelling of the legs or feet. If the symptoms suddenly appear, an immediate medical consultation is needed.
- Being unusually overweight. This usually does not have a medical cause but should always be evaluated by a physician.
- Losing weight, especially if not obviously related to illness or if the child's health is not being supervised by a physician. Preadolescents should not try to lower or seriously control their weight without medical supervision; and adolescents should not diet to lose more than five pounds or so without medical consultation.
- Frequent rapid, jerky movements, especially if in the area of the face or involving the arms or legs. Some jerking when going to sleep is normal.
- Brief or extended periods of blanking out or loss of awareness. Seeing this once or twice warrants medical consultation.
- Fainting or passing out. If this results from getting too hot, it is a medical emergency.
- Numbness of any body part, especially if the child was not cold, in one position too long, or if feeling does not return in five minutes or so.
- General weakness, especially if the child is not ill, tired, or if it involves only one side of the body.
- Unusual staggering or lack of balance.
- Convulsions, seizures, or unusual spells.

CHAPTER 9

CLOSING THOUGHTS

Parental Maladjustment

As you talk with parents, it is important to develop the perspective that, at times, parents' maladjustment can and does negatively affect the adjustment of their kids. Three points here are important. First, parental maladjustment can be as disabling for children as their personal maladjustment. The parents' problems seriously interfere with their children's day-to-day functioning and with their ability to successfully handle life's challenges and opportunities. Second, maladjusted parents are not fully available to their kids. Their problems consume significant personal energy, distract them from their parent role, and lessen their emotional and interpersonal effectiveness. Third, these parents are, to some extent, passing their problems along to their children. Their kids need to adjust to and accommodate to their parent's adjustment difficulties. This means that the children need to spend part of their developmental potential adjusting to parental and family pathology.

This is the point. The children living with maladjusted parents are not receiving the type and level of guidance, nurturing, and encouragement they need and deserve. This deprivation may be minor or may be extreme. Nonetheless, the kids are getting short-changed in the parent department.

When talking with any child's parents, follow the suggestions from the preceding chapters. During the conversation, you may begin to suspect that one (or both) of the parents is having adult maladjustment-related difficulties. If so, do not directly focus your discussion on the adult problems. If the parent shifts the conversation toward the adult problems, say, "I appreciate the importance of the difficulties you (or your spouse) are having. I can see that they concern you. For right now, though, it'll help most to keep our focus on your child. How hard is it going to be for you (and your spouse) to follow through with getting him the help he needs? With all that is going on for you right now, I can see how it won't be easy to do what I'm sure you want to do for your child. Would it help if I helped you make the arrangements for your child to see the specialist we talked about?" Few parents will reject your offer of assistance.[31]

Whether you intuitively suspect a parent maladjustment problem or the parent with whom you are talking brings it up, say, for example, "When your child goes for counseling, a couple things will happen. The counselor will evaluate your child and likely will schedule a few counseling sessions for him. It's also important for you to understand the services he is getting and how you will be participating in his treatment. Usually parents need to make some adjustments in the way they deal with their child, for his treatment to be successful. You should ask to talk with the counselor individually about what you may need to do to best help your child. If you want, I'll call the counselor to be sure she plans on meeting with you to focus on whatever helps you help your child. May I do this for you? I think it may be the best way to be sure your child gets everything he needs." Again, few parents will reject this offer. When you make the arrangements with the specialist, you need only mention your concerns about the parent's adjustment. The counselor will take it from there.

The Heart of Being a Parent

Each child is special. If his parents do not hold this feeling and consistently convey it to him with sincerity and enthusiasm, their child will know and will suffer in proportion. Most parental interaction with children has little if anything to do with encouragement or discouragement, boundaries or limit setting. Rather, parents are participants with their kids in the fun and frustration of learning and growing physically, emotionally, and socially. Parents want their children to love them, to love themselves, to love other people, and to love the world around them. They express their love for their kids through touching, physical involvement, playing, doing things with their children, and through sharing feelings and fears and frustrations. They go places with their kids and want them to go places with them. At the same time, effective parents allow their children the freedom to grow and to experience the

[31]Whether you make the arrangements for specialized services or the parents do it themselves, if you can, check back in a couple of weeks to see how things are going and ask how the arrangements are working out for them and their child. Your interest is supportive and you have a second opportunity to "make the connection" if they have not followed through.

world away from them. Their relationship with their kids is not exclusive. They want them to have an exciting life of their own, knowing that their relationship with their parents is secure and predictable.

In addition, nurturing parents want their children to respect them, to respect themselves, other people, and the world about them. Much of a child's attitude toward himself and toward the world about him comes from his parents' attitudes about him.

Just as children learn to love by being loved, they learn respect for self and others by being respected. Parental behavior, attitudes, and beliefs will, in large measure, be reflected in children. More than we adults may ever know, they "do as we do."

Children also develop attitudes toward themselves and others as a response to the attitudes and beliefs others communicate to them about themselves. In part, kids become what their parents tell them they will become. Parents convey this definition of self through their physical, emotional, and social interactions with their children as well as through the way they relate as responsible adults. Beyond these things, there is a whole world of influences over which parents have little control. Their hope must be that they have encouraged and supported their children's potentials so they can effectively deal with the multiple influences of the world. They can only hope that their loving respect has been strong enough and clear enough to be integrated into the being of their children as they move out into a world that may not perceive them as unique. Kids' sense of being special comes from home. Their parents can only hope it is solid enough to last a lifetime; and through the sensitive and thoughtful advice you provide to their parents, the odds for success will be better for those children through whose lives you pass.

BIBLIOGRAPHY

Adelman, Howard S. *Learning Problems & Learning Disabilities: Moving Forward.* Brooks/Cole, Pacific Grove, CA, 1993.

Barkley, Russell A. *Defiant Children: A Clinician's Manual for Parent Training.* Guilford Press, New York, NY, 1987.

Bender, William N. *Learning Disabilities: Characteristics, Identification and Teaching Strategies.* Allyn and Bacon, Boston, MA, 1995.

Blackman, Garth J., & Silberman, Adolph. *Modification of Child and Adolescent Behavior, 3rd ed.,* Wadsworth, Belmont, CA, 1980.

Braswell, Lauren & Bloomquist, Michael L. *Cognitive-Behavioral Therapy with ADHD Children: Child, Family, and School Interventions.* Guilford Press, New York, NY, 1991.

Brumberg, Joan J. *Fasting Girls: The Emergence of Anorexia Nervosa as a Modern Disease.* Harvard University Press, Cambridge, MA, 1988.

Canino, Ian A. & Spurlock, Jeanne; *Culturally Diverse Children and Adolescents: Assessment, Diagnosis, and Treatment.* Guilford Press, New York, NY, 1994.

Combrinck-Graham, Lee. *Children in Family Contexts: Perspectives on Treatment.* Guilford Press, New York, NY, 1989.

Crow, Gary A. & Crow, Letha I. *Crisis Intervention and Suicide Prevention: Working with Children and Adolescents.* Charles C Thomas, Springfield, IL, 1987.

Crow, Gary A. & Crow, Letha I. *The Functioning of the Family System: A Social Interaction Approach.* Charles C Thomas, Springfield, IL, 1988.

Crow, Gary A. & Crow, Letha I. *Our Home—Your Home.* American Foster Care Resources, King George, VA, 1993.

Cullinan, Douglas., Epstein, Michael H., & Lloyd, John W. *Behavior Disorders of Children and Adolescents.* Prentice-Hall, Englewood Cliffs, NJ, 1983.

Dodds, Josiah B. *A Child Psychotherapy Primer: Suggestions For the Beginning Therapist.* Human Sciences Press, New York, NY, 1987.

Elkind, David. *The Hurried Child: Growing Up Too Fast Too Soon.* Addison-Wesley, Reading, MA, 1988.

Garber, Stephen W., Garber, Marianne D. & Spizman, Robyn F. *Good Behavior: Over 1,200 Sensible Solutions to Your Child's Problems From Birth to Age Twelve.* Villard Books, New York, NY, 1987.

Garfinkel, Barry D., Carlson, Gabrielle A. & Weller, Elizabeth B. *Psychiatric Disorders in Children and Adolescents.* W. B. Saunders, Philadelphia, PA, 1990.

Greenspan, Stanley I. & Salmon, Jacqueline. *The Challenging Child: Understanding,*

Raising, and Enjoying the Five "Difficult" Types of Children. Addison-Wesley, Reading, MA, 1995.

Holt, John C. *How Children Learn.* Delta/Seymour Lawrence, New York, NY, 1983.

Kauffman, James M. *Characteristics of Children's Behavior Disorders, 2nd ed.* Charles E. Merrill, Columbus, OH, 1981.

Kendall, Philip C. & Braswell, Lauren. *Cognitive-Behavioral Therapy for Impulsive Children.* Guilford Press, New York, NY, 1985.

McCoy, Kathleen. *Coping with Teenage Depression: A Parent's Guide.* New American Library, New York, NY, 1982.

McNamara, Barry E. & McNamara, Francine J. *Keys to Parenting a Child with a Learning Disability.* Barron's, Hauppauge, NY, 1995.

Meinhold, Patricia. *Child Psychology: Development and Behavior Analysis, 1st ed.* Hunt, Dubuque, IA, 1993.

Mordock, John B. *Counseling Children: Basic Principles for Helping the Troubled and Defiant Child.* Continuum, New York, NY, 1991.

Reisman, John M. *Behavior Disorders in Infants, Children and Adolescents.* Random House, New York, NY, 1986.

Reynolds, Cecil R. & Kamphaus, Randy W. *BASC, Behavior Assessment System for Children.* American Guidance Service, Circle Pines, MN, 1992.

Samenow, Stantone. *Before It's Too Late: Why Some Kids Get Into Trouble—And What Parents Can do About It. (1st ed.)* Times Books, New York, NY, 1989.

Sears, William. *Creative Parenting: How to Use the New Continuum Concept to Raise Children Successfully from Birth Through Adolescence.* Dodd, Mead, New York, NY, 1982.

Silver, Larry B. *The Misunderstood Child: A Guide for Parents of Learning Disabled Children.* McGraw-Hill, New York, NY, 1988.

Steinhauer, Paul D. & Rae-Grant, Quentin. *Psychological Problems of the Child in the Family.* Basic Books, New York, NY, 1983.

Taylor, John F. *Helping Your Hyperactive, Attention Deficit Child.* Prima, Rocklin, CA, 1994.

Thompson, Charles L. & Rudolph, Linda B. *Counseling Children.* Brooks/Cole, Pacific Grove, CA, 1992.

Turecki, Stanley & Tonner, Leslie. *The Difficult Child.* Bantam Books, New York, NY, 1989.

Vail, Priscilla L. *Smart Kids with School Problems: Things To Know and Ways to Help.* E. P. Dutton, New York, NY, 1987.

Walker, C. E. & Roberts, Michael C. *Handbook of Clinical Child Psychology.* John Wiley & Sons, New York, NY, 1983.

Weisberg, Lynne W. & Greenberg, Rosalie. *When Acting Out Isn't Acting: Understanding Child and Adolescent Temper, Anger and Behavior Disorders.* PIA Press, Washington, DC, 1988.

Zirpoli, Thomas J. & Melloy, Kristine J. *Behavior Management: Applications for Teachers and Parents.* Merrill, New York, NY, 1993.